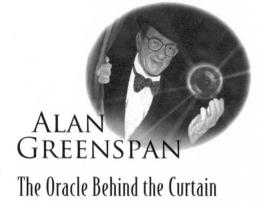

ALAN GREENSPAN

The Oracle Behind the Curtain

ALAN GREENSPAN

The Oracle Behind the Curtain

E. Ray Canterbery

Florida State University, USA

World Scientific

NEW JERSEY · LONDON · SINGAPORE · BEIJING · SHANGHAI · HONG KONG · TAIPEI · CHENNAI

Published by

World Scientific Publishing Co. Pte. Ltd.

5 Toh Tuck Link, Singapore 596224

USA office: 27 Warren Street, Suite 401-402, Hackensack, NJ 07601

UK office: 57 Shelton Street, Covent Garden, London WC2H 9HE

British Library Cataloguing-in-Publication Data
A catalogue record for this book is available from the British Library.

ALAN GREENSPAN
The Oracle Behind the Curtain

ISBN 981-256-606-6

Typeset by Stallion Press
Email: enquiries@stallionpress.com

Printed in Singapore by Mainland Press

CONTENTS

A PERSONAL NOTE

Alan Greenspan: The Oracle Behind the Curtain is a sequel to my *Wall Street Capitalism (WSC)*. As at the movies, however, it is quite different from the original. Apropos, people in the global community, especially businesspeople and economists, view Greenspan as a celebrity. True, his face is one of the most recognizable on earth—a deeply-etched face that reflects a gravitas beyond timeless gravity. The only musical celebrity with competitive wrinkles is Mick Jagger who went to the London School of Economics on a scholarship before dropping out to become a rock star. Greenspan graduated summa cum laude, with a B.S. in economics from New York University; later, he dropped out of graduate school to become a Jazz musician. Now, it is difficult to tell who is the bigger star, though now in reversed fields. Greenspan is the conductor of money policy.

Greenspan's fame has led to titles as varied as maestro, wizard, oracle, and the Pope of Wall Street. His public image conveys all such job descriptions, so we will alternate these identities. Of celebrities like the London School drop-out, Greenspan's fame will last more than the proverbial fifteen minutes on the world stage. In this way, his celebrity status is a reflection of his powers—past, present and future. As with rock stars, people generally know more about Greenspan's personal life than his professional tricks; *unlike* our intimate knowledge of rock stars, we know little. For example, we know that Greenspan likes to take notes every morning in the bathtub before hurrying off to give a speech whether it be as head of the Federal Reserve or otherwise, but we may never know what he meant when he said "hedge funds are strongly regulated by those who lend the money." Or, will we?

So, this volume is different from *WSC* in several respects, but not simply for the new entertainment content. Why different? In abject honesty, some earlier warnings bear repeating and updating because the dangers to the U.S. and the global economy have seldom been greater. With more than adequate discomfort, I have come to the same conclusion as in *WSC* and in my *The Making of Economics*—namely, that ideology is often more powerful and decisive than reason. Alan Greenspan, as his unique kind of celebrity, has a lot to do with it. His economic and political powers likely will not only be preserved, but also extended. These powers and his legacy would be minimal absent ideology and Alan's lifetime success promoting a free market ideology. After all, we live in an age when The Market has become God and creationism is being touted as on equal footing with the science of evolution. Alan Greenspan is not a religious man, *except* for his devout belief in The Market. History's most renowned central banker sees markets as science present at the Creation, and has difficulty separating *his* church from state.

Cynicism would be the easy but unproductive path to understanding the powers that are Greenspan and that have defined the American central bank. I have gleaned Greenspan and the Fed's history mostly from public records, while the social satire and good humor is of my own creation, though having evolved over the years.

E. Ray Canterbery

ONWARD

Newswires are atwitter. The CNBC morning business news team members always speak in quick, excited voices when any Federal Reserve news is about to made. Or, in truth, every twitch in a stock price, quarterly earnings report or interest rate elicits animated behavior far out of proportion to the size of the spasm. Rick Santelli at CNBC can bring the same drama even to the bond market. This could have one of any number of days. This day, however—even for breaking business news—is special. It is the third weekend in June 2004.

Alan Greenspan is sworn in as chair of the Federal Reserve Board of Governors for an *unprecedented* fifth term. The degree of excitement is exceptional despite its long-awaited inevitability. News reports at his Papal-like "election" say that Greenspan has told friends that he will "retire" at the end of January 2006. Although the Fed's chair is nominated by the President and senatorially confirmed (with minimal opposition), no president has acted as if he had a choice regarding Greenspan's re-appointment. Once appointed, in any case, the chair answers to neither the president of the United States, the Congress nor anyone else.

What Mr. Greenspan told his friends suggests that he considers "retirement" from the chairmanship as voluntary. According to current law, however, a Governor who serves a full term can't be reappointed. Since Greenspan originally took office as Chairman to fill an unexpired term as a member of the Board on August 11, 1987, his full fourteen-year term as a Governor did not began until February 1, 1992, and does end January 31, 2006. His "retirement" nonetheless is not as inevitable as his appointment. The oracle of monetary policy has an enviable record of predictable retirement statements preceding presidential elections. It was always a hedge, reflecting perhaps

Greenspan's inside knowledge of those mysterious hedge funds. If the president of the United States can't find an "acceptable chair" by the end of January and names Greenspan as interim chairman, he could stay on until 2008. Opposition from the U.S. Senate is unlikely.

At the time of Alan Greenspan's first appointment as chair, the stock market Crash of 1987 was still ringing in the ears of Wall Street; Ronald Reagan was president. Greenspan was reappointed to another term by another Republican president, H.W. George Bush. When Bill Clinton, a Democrat, became president in 1993, Greenspan had several years left to his term. Still, Clinton was put under tremendous pressure by Wall Street to reappoint Greenspan when his term expired and did so in 1996 and again in 2000, even though Greenspan is a Republican. By an early promise to retire, Greenspan had preempted the decision of any president who might next be elected or "appointed." In 2000, George W. Bush (Rep.) was "appointed" president by the U.S. Supreme Court. George W. and Greenspan have something else in common; both are *very* conservative Republicans and master politicians.

Greenspan turned seventy-nine in March 2005. He has been in excellent health for his age and is renowned for playing tennis and golf with men as young as Ben Benanke, a Federal Reserve Board Governor—later, head of W's Council of Economic Advisers and, then, the nominee for Greenspan's job. While showing some physical signs of aging, Greenspan's mental acuity—especially in the morning hours—remains remarkable. He is known for retiring, only as in "going to bed," at very early times.

In national politics Alan Greenspan has been more, or less than head of the Reserve. George W. Bush is the *sixth* U.S. President, beginning with Richard Nixon, served by Greenspan either as an economic advisor or as head of the Fed. As a libertarian but sometimes orthodox Republican, Alan's nasal monotone and lugubrious demeanor has been comforting to the rich. The poor generally don't know him while the middle class does not understand him. Too many Americans don't have a clue as to what he does, an ignorance that the Federal Reserve and Greenspan have always preferred, even cultivated, and will likely continue to prefer and cultivate.

As to the truth, while the rich may know Dr. Greenspan, most rich people don't know what the Fed does either; they don't need to. Greenspan and they have never seen a market or a bank merger they didn't like. Most central bankers do not socialize with poor persons; if Greenspan ever did, this unlikely knight (knighted by Queen Elizabeth) would likely be insensate to the condition of poverty since he presumes it to be self-inflicted. While some rich folk are liberals or left-wing Darth Vadars to neoconservatives, those most influential during the past quarter-century and counting are from the conservative dark side.

Much in American culture and science has changed if we travel back to when Greenspan was appointed chair of the Reserve by Reagan; the *Simpson's* were debuting on TV and Americans were living in the Prozac Nation. Later, Greenspan was caricatured on *The Simpson's*. Now, it is claimed by wealth holders and political conservatives that Greenspan has become as indispensable to the United States (and perhaps the world) as Queen Victoria was to the Victorian Age. If so, he indeed is irreplaceable.

During these decades Mr. Greenspan has accumulated incredible amounts of political capital, more even than Bush II; as chair of the Fed he has been in total control of monetary policy. The Fed has been operating on a Greenspan Standard as solidly as Queen Victoria operated on a Gold Standard during the nineteenth century. The chairman's assessment of not only financial policies but of all things even remotely related to the economy rules the day. When he goes, however, he would like the Greenspan Standard preserved; if not, the Gold Standard revived.

Meanwhile, the Fed has received stellar reviews; these reviews, however, are suspect. The unique combination of Greenspan's political capital, politicians reluctance to challenge the Fed, a press corps willingness to trade glowing reviews for access, and private economists who all dream of possibly becoming Fed Governors or at least members of the Federal Reserve staff, assures an endless supply of get-out-of-jail-free cards for the Fed. We will come to know the foundation of this immense political power, the source of such free passes.

Uniquely, the Federal Reserve enjoys an absence of checks and balances strongly preferred and nearly achieved by administrations such as

those of Richard Nixon and George W. Bush. The Fed is both a part of
government and apart from government. It is that great oxymoron, a
"quasi-public" institution or in politically-correct free market nomen-
clature, "quasi-private." Alan Greenspan, who generally has had his
way with the economy, has not seriously considered it either—rather,
to him, the Fed is simply "quasi." As to the truth of what Greenspan
does, it is as mundane as it is remarkable: he sets short-term interest
rates for the American economy. He has been able to raise or lower
such rates willy-nilly. He also is the czar of American financial markets
extended in many realms to global markets.

Though repetition is, well, boring, it sometimes serves clarity. While
it is true that a handful of die-hard "monetarist" and "supply-side"
economists believe that the nation's money supply, variously and repet-
itively defined, decides everything, it is a mistaken view to which we will
return, only for proper burial. The interest rate or its plural is the only
tool of monetary policy, though the Federal Reserve can engage business, the economy and society in other ways—or not. We will consider
both what is done and what is not.

Despite all of the above, Greenspan and the Fed have been immune
to criticism. Greenspan is the subject of several biographies, virtually
all worshipful. Aiding and abetting his persona is a quarter century
of neoconservative political successes. Liberal has become a four-letter
word for those who do count but can't. With all the remarkably favorable opinion that Greenspan has enjoyed, surely an economist who has
a satirical take on the Federal Reserve and Greenspan is taking a huge
risk. The risk is worth taking because Greenspan's successor will inherit
the same powers that Greenspan has enjoyed and even expanded. It is
important not only to understand those powers but why they are so
resistant to moderation. That it took 455 years to pry the papacy out
of Italian hands and into those of a pope from Poland is sobering.
Just as John Paul II's legacy for the Catholic Church, for better or for
worse, will be long-lasting, so too will be the legacy of the Pope of Wall
Street. In this, there is much at stake—not just for Americans, but also
for people around the world. Besides, no immunization exists for satire.

In a democracy no public official is supposed to be immune from
criticism. That Alan Greenspan probably considers himself a private

official with public responsibilities does not alter this condition; rather, it makes scrutiny imperative. He too is a formidable target. He has been cross-examined by members of the Congress on a regular basis; but also, it is fair to say, no one in Congress has been able to lay so much as a blue suede golf glove on him. He is effective in such public forums and is his own best defender. He is, in short, a worthy adversary. This aspect of his personality and abilities, I grant. In a sense I am only adding text to the Oliphant and Toles' cartoons that grace this book.

To begin, I offer only one example of the presumed infallibility of Alan Greenspan. The year 1989 is pivotal in our story. In that year Greenspan hiked the federal funds rate target to nine point seven five percent and the real (inflation-adjusted) funds rate hit five percent. A recession followed, beginning in July 1990. This recession and Bush I's loss of the 1990 presidential election are widely blamed on Saddam Hussein's invasion of Kuwait and rising oil prices. No one, including members of the American press, seems to remember that Iraq did not invade Kuwait until *August*, a month *after* the Fed-induced recession began. Mr. H.W. George Bush was the exceptional U.S. president who blamed Greenspan for a loss of what once was the most powerful office in the world; it was not the first or the last such losses at the hands of Fed policies or of Greenspan. Unlike the press, we will come to know many more instances of Greenspan-inflicted damages. Ironically, Presidents of the United States have fallen because of Federal Reserve policies, while the institution and Alan Greenspan go marching on.

1

GREENSPAN AND THE MYTH
OF HIS PURITY

"Gold," writes Greenspan, "is the ultimate weapon of the haves against inflation," a way for the "owners of wealth" to "protect" themselves against government schemes to "confiscate the wealth of the productive members of society to support a wide variety of welfare schemes."

Alan Greenspan, "Gold and Economic Freedom,"
The Objectivist, July 1966, reprinted in Ayn Rand,
Capitalism: The Unknown Ideal (New York: Signet Books).

Alan Greenspan has been the single most powerful figure affecting the global economy since 1987. He had substantial influence before then as an economic adviser to Presidents Richard M. Nixon and Gerald Ford. Even retired, he will remain an important political force. He has been called apolitical, someone so detached from politics that he can always be trusted. Above all, he is the detached observer subservient to no political motive or operative. He is *pure*. He wants also to maintain *the purity* of the Federal Reserve System so as to insulate the Fed from the influence of politicians, who surely cannot be trusted.

Greenspan's purity—as with most self-consciously persistent claims—is a myth. Moreover, as we will come to know, the purity of the Federal Reserve System is a sham. In the instance of Mr. Greenspan, "purity" generally has meant selfless dedication to an objective view of economic conditions untarnished by decisions benefiting special interests. To the contrary, we best understand this wizard behind the veil of money through a realistic understanding of his aims as well as the supra-natural instincts of the Federal Reserve System. But, first, let us consider Greenspan.

1

Greenspan's policies have always been directed at the protection of the greatest financial wealth holders. Whether it is dealing with stock market bubbles, currency crises or the bailout of giant financial institutions, his actions and those of the Federal Reserve generally have been forces shifting the income and wealth of Americans toward the top and away from the bottom and middle classes. Only through this prism can his policy positions and those inherited by his successor be understood. These effects go beyond the United States; it is a global strategy carried out not only though the Fed, but through multinational financial institutions, including the International Monetary Fund, the World Bank and private hedge funds. The Federal Reserve and the wizard have a unified defense for such policies: A central bank can't influence the configurations of family incomes and wealth. This is simply and categorically wrong.

Maestro Greenspan's background ideally prepared him for his historic conducting of monetary policy. From his early days in New York City he quietly groomed himself for the uncompromising ideological stance he would take. Because of the imprint he leaves at the Federal Reserve, a shift in direction will require two things: the selection of a chair of opposite ideological leanings (unlikely in the age of President George W. Bush) and a severing of the intimate ties of the American central bank to the American and global financial community. Because of the co-dependency of the two—the setting of financial policy by the Fed and the use of financial markets to conduct these policies—institutional reform will require progressive forces at least as strong and effective as present day neoconservatism. We turn now to the maestro, the wizard, the oracle, and the Pope's inevitability.

Young Greenspan: The Musician and Keynesian

Alan Greenspan has never been quite as dull as he appears. His first career was as a musician, once even playing professionally with a 1940s swing band. Alan entered famed Juilliard as a clarinet major in the winter of 1943, but left the first week of the next year to play in Henry Jerome's swing band. Jerome's band was several notches below those of Benny Goodman, Glenn Miller, or Artie Shaw. Jerome played the "businessman's bounce," more Guy Lombardo than Artie Shaw, at un-hip places. It didn't matter; the swing era was coming to an end by the mid-1940s.

Jerome switched to bebop late in 1944—a new craze pioneered by Dizzy Gillespie, Charlie Parker and others. With its new hip style Jerome's new band attracted several very talented young musicians, but the band never made it in the record business mostly because of a wartime shellac shortage required for the old-fashioned 78 rpm records. Henry Jerome' band *dis*banded in 1945, with Greenspan quitting a few months ahead of Jerome. While Greenspan was a pretty good amateur musician, he was only average as a professional. It was like the difference between playing golf under the USGA and the PGA.

OLIPHANT © (2001) UNIVERSAL PRESS SYNDICATE. Reprinted with permission. All rights reserved.

Greenspan, the "Keynesian," is even more difficult to conjure up than Greenspan, the jazz musician. Always a bookish sort, Greenspan next enrolled in New York University's School of Commerce, and was among the few pursuing a degree in economics. One of the first economics books that Greenspan read on his own was Dudley Dillard's *The Economics of J. M. Keynes*, perhaps the best popular exposition of Keynes' work. In Keynes' *General Theory* [1936], a government could end a business recession or depression by spending more than its tax revenue—willingly running federal budget deficits, a very radical idea at the time. It not only became Franklin Roosevelt's fiscal program during the Great Depression, but was the policy choice to fight business downturns of most economists until Reaganomics hit the fan.

Greenspan, seemingly impressionable, soon would be persuaded that Dillard, Keynes and Roosevelt were wrong. Geoffrey Moore, one of Greenspan's teachers, assigned *Measuring Business Cycles* by Arthur Burns and Wesley Mitchell [1946]. Moore, an incurable collector of economic data, developed a leading indicator of economic activity that Greenspan would later use in his work. Then, when young Alan went to graduate school at Columbia University, Arthur Burns was one of his professors and ultimately, his mentor. Burns, initially noted for hair parted down the middle, large round wire-rimmed glasses and a ubiquitous pipe, became one of the few critics of John Maynard Keynes at the time. Burns was asking Greenspan's class: "What causes inflation?" While his students remained silent, Burns' answered with a slap in Keynes' face, "Excess government spending causes inflation."

Arthur Burns' powerful personality was sufficient to turn young Greenspan into the staunch supporter of laissez-faire and limited government that neoconservatives around the globe have grown to love. As we will come to know, this is unfortunate. Eventually, Burns' free market credentials would eventually guarantee him the chairmanship of the Federal Reserve System where he would instill the fear of inflation from government deficits in American minds.

Greenspan's Randy Past

The switch from jazz musician to economist, from liberal Keynesianism to conservative laissez-faire political economy, would not be Greenspan's final reversals. Ten months after a blind date with Joan Mitchell—an extraordinary blond in her early twenties, elegant and highly cultured—they were married. Alan had dropped out of Columbia because he was having trouble coming up with the tuition. Besides, Arthur Burns had gone to Washington to serve as chairman of the Council of Economic Advisers (CEA) in the Eisenhower administration. Greenspan went to work at what was then the National Industrial Conference Board, later shortened to the Conference Board, a not-for-profit business research organization. Meanwhile, Joan was spending a lot of time with a group of New York "intellectuals" interested in a philosophy called objectivism. Alan and Joan drifted apart and their marriage was annulled in 1953. Joan became a good friend post-annulment.

With the end of his marriage, Greenspan did a turnabout on objectivism; he had hated it when married to Joan but grew to admire Ayn Rand, the feisty woman behind the philosophy. ("Ayn" rimes with "swine," as an amused Rand reminded people.) From Greenspan's late twenties to his early forties, objectivism was a major part of his life, as he spent many hours in the company of Rand and her narrow circle, sufficiently wide nonetheless to make his head spin. She was to have as much influence on Alan as Arthur Burns. And, she did not even part her hair in the middle—rather, she wore bangs. Ayn Rand was formidable: she was brilliant, charismatic, iconoclastic, logical to the point of insanity, and capable of dramatic displays of incendiary temper. Some claim that she was mentally ill.

Greenspan Joins the Radical Right Collective

By now, Alan Greenspan was well to the political right of the Eisenhower Republicans. He still is. As for Dwight D. Eisenhower, Ayn Rand considered him a closet communist. As for Greenspan, he became one of the first students at the Nathaniel Branden Institute, the "think tank" founded by Rand's lover to further her ideas. Rand called Greenspan "the undertaker" because—among other things—he always dressed in a black suit matching his demeanor, much like the one he wore to her funeral. He also was a bit of a pessimist who was not sure that he could prove he existed. Greenspan, as Fed chair, took to wearing only blue, perhaps so he would seem less the villain to blue-collar workers.

Greenspan was a member of a radical right group known to themselves as the Collective and, to Rand, as the Class of '43, modestly named for the year of her novel, *The Fountainhead*. Summing theologically the Collective's philosophy, Rand evokes radical individualism as the theme of *The Fountainhead*, which she called "individualism versus collectivism, not in politics, but in man's soul." Its hero, architect Howard Roark (Gary Cooper in the film), embodies a philosophy of pure self-interest. He designs a gigantic government housing project for the poor only under the condition that he designs it *his way* (*this* before Frank Sinatra's recording). In the end, Roark cannot save the project from the many evil-doers opposing him in the name of some greater good, such as the Robinhoodesque-taking from the rich and giving to the poor. Thus, Roark is justified in destroying his butchered creation with a charge of dynamite! The poorly housed are left with rubble, but Roark has saved Rand's philosophical theme: the evil "do-gooders" put the heroic entrepreneur in the awkward but defensible position of having to blow up their project.

The Collective converted Greenspan into a lover of free markets, a man not only suspicious of do-gooders but having a righteous hatred of government. No doubt Alan came under the spell of objectivism's narrow focus on rationality and individualism. Under this new philosophy, Greenspan was able to convince himself that he did, indeed, exist. Once converted, Rand came to admire Alan; now they both were fellow radicals for capitalism. In 1974 Greenspan tells *Newsweek*: "When I met Ayn Rand, I was a free enterpriser in the Adam Smith sense, impressed with the theoretical structure and efficiency of markets. What she did was to make me see that capitalism is not only efficient and practical, but also moral." He had become a moralist.

Greenspan helped Rand with some of her research for her next novel, *Atlas Shrugged*. While *The Fountainhead* had been about architecture, her new novel would be about the world of heavy, *really* heavy industry. Not only did Greenspan know much about railroads, oil derricks and steel mills, he now occupied a heavy role in the Collective. On top, of course, was Rand, followed by Nathaniel Branden, then Barbara Branden, *then* Greenspan. Bennett Cerf, an editor faced with a novel of 645,000 words, suggested that perhaps a few words could be cut. "Would you cut the Bible?" was Ayn Rand's cutting reply. The reviews, such as "The worst piece of fiction since *The Fountainhead*," were savage. In response to a scathing review by Granville Hicks in the *New York Times*, Alan Greenspan was moved to write an angry letter (published November 3, 1957) in which he wondered "about a person who finds unrelenting justice personally disturbing."

Still, passionate devotees were found for *The Fountainhead* and *Atlas Shrugged*. Enough that in 1958 Nathaniel Branden was able to found his modestly named Nathaniel Branden Institute. It opened with a series of twenty lectures called "Basic Principles of Objectivism." Greenspan developed a ninety-minute lecture entitled "The Economics of a Free Society" that would make Ronald Reagan's General Electric speech on free enterprise appear to be a communist manifesto. Eventually there would be a magazine called the *Objectivist*; Greenspan was a frequent contributor.

The Short Distances from Rand to Wall Street to Washington, D.C.

Greenspan certainly never wandered far from his Randian roots or from Wall Street, a short walk away. In 1954 he and an older bond trader, William Townsend, established the New York-based consulting firm Townsend-Greenspan & Company. The company not only made Greenspan a millionaire (when it meant something), but also introduced him to the biggest banks in New York. At Ayn Rand's aggressive prodding, Greenspan entered the political arena as the director of domestic policy research for Richard Nixon's 1968 presidential campaign. Staying on as an informal Nixon adviser, the future central banker easily bridged the ideological gap between Wall Street and Washington. From Townsend, Greenspan learned how inflationary expectations could depress bond prices and increase long-term interest rates, something he never forgot.

The volatile mixture of Randian philosophy, Wall Street values and Washington reality, nonetheless sometimes exploded. For instance, Greenspan created a problem for Nixon by setting in motion a proposal to free Wall Street from regulations. Since many on Main Street didn't trust Wall Street and still don't, the idea of regulating Wall Street was very unpopular. Nixon had to reverse Greenspan. Still, the president asked a seemingly reluctant Greenspan to head the president's Council of Economic Advisers. What happened next was fortuitous, for Greenspan had little admiration for Nixon's dark side. About the time of Greenspan's appointment, Nixon was forced to resign under a cloud of impeachment and the future maestro was named President Gerald Ford's chief economic adviser.

Ayn Rand came down from New York, along with her hard-drinking, long-suffering husband, Frank O'Connor, for Greenspan's inaugural ceremony, September 4, 1974. For Rand, Greenspan's appointment comprised some vindication for her beliefs; someone from her small circle was in a position of power, which she called "a heroic undertaking"—much like Howard Roark in a black suit. Alan Greenspan's invitation of Rand to the ceremony was itself heroic, testimony to his fervent belief in her doctrines. Greenspan, a born-again opponent of government and now the chief economic adviser to the president, moved into the Old Executive Office Building wonderfully situated next to the White House.

2

ADAM SMITH, FREE MARKETS AND THE GREENSPAN STANDARD

When the conversation turns to central bankers at what were once called cocktail parties, people always ask: What kind of economist is Alan Greenspan? In truth, people don't talk about central banking at parties or even orgies, unless they are held in Washington, D.C. or on Wall Street. With all the importance of American central bankers, perhaps fifteen to thirty minutes should be set aside for just such a discussion. Besides, the answer to the Greenspan question is more intriguing and surprising than most people imagine. By the standards of any academy of economists, Greenspan, the wizened wizard of money, is not an economist at all.

Mr. Greenspan did not receive his Ph.D. from New York University (NYU) until 1977, almost three decades after his undergraduate degree but also after his stint as head of the President's Council of Economic Advisers (CEA). While the average age of a Ph.D. economist is around thirty years at graduation, none have enrolled at the age of zero. Worse, Alan never finished his dissertation, normally a requirement. Rather, his degree was awarded on the "strength" of articles Greenspan had published in a variety of popular magazines and journals beginning in 1959 plus a document he had written as CEA chairman, an *Economic Report of the U.S. President*. The collection, "Papers on Economic Theory and Policy," might be considered adequate for a Ph.D. from a diploma mill in the Bahamas. Still, Barbara Walters of TV fame had an intimate party at her apartment in Manhattan to toast the new Dr. Greenspan.

Controversy surrounds Greenspan's Ph.D., not so much because of Barbara Walters' little party, but for substantial reasons. The dissertation substitute was not meritorious, especially since the *Economic Report* was one of the most ideological ever written. A long tradition of academic openness and accessibility requires that anyone— be they taxi driver or professor, or both—can drive into a university and read Ph.D. dissertations. The demand on librarians is not onerous because most such works are dry tomes carefully avoided. Dr. Greenspan uniquely requested that NYU withhold from public view his "Papers on Economic Theory and Policy." A decade later, as head of the Fed, such concealment would continue to serve Greenspan well, as it has central bankers before him, and perhaps those ever afterward.

There is nothing inherently wrong with practicing economics with a suspect license. As in any field, only a few authentic Ph.D. economists can claim brilliance. Still fewer are so talented as to make a Ph.D. irrelevant. The greatest of the British economists such as John Maynard Keynes and Joan Robinson did not have Ph.D.'s, nor did Isaac Newton. To judge a central banker's actions, it is nonetheless useful to know their economic philosophy or what kind of "economist" they are. Already, we have identified Greenspan's Randian ideology and that is sufficient.

The Inflation Hawk and the Greenspan Standard

We begin with the way Alan Greenspan was, which turns out to be the way he mostly is. During the mid-1970s, the future chairman is an inflation hawk with a very wide wingspan: "If inflation continues, our system will not hold together in its present form," he suggests in fall 1974. At one of the mini-summits on the broad state of the economy on September 19, 1974, Jerry Wurf, then president of the American Federation of State County and Municipal Employees, states that Ford's policies favor rich bankers over poor citizens. "Mr. Wurf," Greenspan replies, "we all have an interest in this economy. If someone believes that there is some way that someone is not hurt by inflation, ... If you really wanted to examine who percentage-wise is hurt the most in their incomes, it is the Wall Street brokers. I mean their incomes have gone down the most. So if you want to get statistical, I mean let's look at what the facts are." Greenspan was correct about who would be hurt the most by inflation: It would be the Wall Street fat cat with the fullest wallet and the most income to lose. It was one of those rare moments when Greenspan vocalized clearly who he was most concerned about. He would become quite subtle thereafter, but never change his mind.

It was not long before the hawk's beak of Greenspan began to peck away at the inflation monster. Greenspan proposed a sharp reduction in government spending during the presidential election year of 1976, presumably to douse the flames of inflationary expectations, which were feeding increases in long-term interest rates. As the country entered its deepest recession in fourteen years, Greenspan somehow persuaded presidential candidate Ford (now running on his own steam) to ignore recession and attack the inflationary menace at a time when unemployment already stood at eight percent! To be fair, Ford too feared inflation more than unemployment; after all, he was a golf-club carrying Republican. Voters were unsympathetic; they elected peanut-farmer Jimmy Carter president. Greenspan himself was involuntarily unemployed from government for a time, returning nonetheless to his high-priced consulting work; he never became a digit in the natural rate of unemployment, as economists began to call it.

While Greenspan has never strayed from his doctrinaire defense of the rich from the poor, he did begin to state it with less clarity. Like his preference for the Gold Standard, his later recommendation to privatize social security and make other changes to "save it" is rooted in his view of social security as an immoral income transfer from wealth holders to the poor. In other essays he attacks antitrust and consumer protections laws. Later, also, in a thinly veiled attack on the government's case against Microsoft in 1998, Greenspan displays a deep philosophical doubt about antitrust enforcement. He says, "I would like to see far more firm roots to our judgments as to whether particular market positions do, in fact, undercut competition or are only presumed on the basis of some generalized judgment of how economic forces are going to evolve." But, he adds, there "ought to be a higher degree of humility" when enforcers make such projections. When Greenspan raises or lowers the fed funds rate target, the overnight lending rate among private banks controlled by th _____ vertheless lacks, if anything, humility.

Still, given Greenspan's track _____ ᵔord, there is adequate room for humility. _____ ᵔrays have been disasters. He wants _____ had not even served the ninete _____ Wall Street that has alw _____ u-lation. Greensr _____ economy is _____ In the rarified _____ best politicians _____ quick to exhale. Fa _____ path to success and p _____ ᵔr. In this respect Greenspa _____ ny of lesser gods.

There is no contradiction _____ in the gold standard, business deregulation _____ practical matter, Greenspan understands that coun _____ back on the gold standard—for dastardly narrow polit _____ is, in his mind. What, then, is the next best thing? It is for A _____ Greenspan to manage the world's money supply and interest rates without interference. That is to say, once in power Greenspan considers his *judgment* to be the *new* gold standard. The Greenspan Standard is to leave markets alone except when the dominant wealth holders require rescue from the market's harsh punishment. Not surprisingly, the wealthy and those on Wall Street agree with him. Whatever irony attends a free-marketeer ultimately becoming the world's most powerful bureaucrat running Washington's most powerful bureaucracy is exculpated by the revelation that Greenspan, the Howard Roark of central banking, is the lonely hero freeing Wall Street and *all markets* from the chains of government. Would he—faithful to the Roark metaphor—also be willing to destroy Wall Street to save it? That is a good question.

The Efficient Market and God

Finance experts have a unique language which they share with central bankers. Most have praised *unregulated* financial markets for their "efficiency." In the efficient financial market the price of the asset is not only always correct, it reflects market fundamentals (though not everyone agrees about what those are). The price of, say Marvel Technologies stock always clears the market; the amounts supplied and demanded of the stock are equal and set the correct price because all the players in the market are rational. How do we know that say $30, is the correct price? Well, it is because $30 is *the* price. If you can't understand this condition, you are not rational. Sorry.

For the financial players and wealth holders there are consequences from market efficiency. A single player in the market, such as financial genius George Soros or investment-guru Warren Buffett (or even a pirate like Jimmy Buffett) can never beat the market. Whatever the market knows is already embedded in Marvel Tech's stock price and Soros or Buffet can't know what the market knows before it knows it because it already knew it. Worse, Soros or Buffet can't know what the market will know in the future because the market already knows that too. Efficiency leads to the notion that all market players should diversify; by essentially holding enough securities as to resemble the market, the player will do no worse than it, but no better. No wonder they think that The Market is God! If we were to point out that Soros and Buffet have made huge fortunes in various financial markets by buying low and selling high, we would be criticized for confusing facts with theory.

Adam Smith, Alan Greenspan and Say's Law

Alan Greenspan embraces the illusion of free markets and their undeniable efficiency as a matter of faith. Not surprisingly, most fans of Alan find an easy association of Adam Smith with Greenspan and other central bankers.

Closely related to the perfection found in markets is a key principle of the ideology of Alan Greenspan: personal savings magically become real business investment in machine tools and factories, investment that will make workers better-off. The idea is not original; the names of Adam Smith and J. B. Say have been most often invoked in support of this view. By lifting this idea out of its proper historical context, converting it to idealized eighteenth-century dogma, Wall Street and

Greenspan try to justify low income taxes and low capital gains taxes for the rich and high tax rates on those who work for a living.

To Smith is attributed the importance of laissez-faire, by which the only proper role for government in the economy is to make the city streets safe for businessmen. With the invisible hand at work in markets, capitalism is as self-regulating as the planetary system. In this utopia no business cycle and no unemployment (except that which is voluntary) could happen. In freshman economics we are taught that Adam Smith instructed the world about the way markets magically self-adjust, only to ascend to higher planes and to the betterment of all. Smith not only imbues capital accumulation with high morality as it is "increased by parsimony and diminished by prodigality," but believed that all savings become real capital investment. As he put it, "what is annually saved is as regularly consumed as what is annually spent, and nearly in the same time too; but it is consumed by a different set of people." The "consumption" by the second "set of people" is of capital goods such as horse and plows for the Scottish farmers and store fronts for the merchants.

Later, in 1803 the idea was popularized by a French journalist, J. B. Say, and became known as Say's law whereby personal savings bringing about an equal value of real business investment prevented "general gluts" or economy-wide surpluses. In good time Say's law got embedded in Wall Street ideology and eventually in a financial markets strategy derived by Greenspan during the Clinton administration. However, Smith's grand vision was how to get the engine of growth started, a natural for his times; it had little relevance for advanced capitalism or even for the Industrial Revolution following but not anticipated by Adam Smith.

In Adam Smith's view, to repeat, individual or personal savings not only generate real investment but the two are always equal despite their generation by two different sets of people. Wage earners and peasants could not afford to save; at best they would earn a living wage, enough to feed and house them so they could go back to work another day. Only the rich, those with incomes greater than that required for buying necessities, could "afford" to save. Because of the direction of effects—from savings causing investment—the social purpose of the rich is elevated to uncommon heights. This transmutation of savings into real capital assures full employment in a free market economy. In the investment banking houses of Wall Street, the prosperity, even the survival, of capitalism depends greatly on higher incomes and greater savings by the rich. It is a socially convenient myth for a wealth holding class of which Greenspan is not only a member but a fan.

Still later, David Ricardo (1772–1823), once a stockbroker and member of the British Parliament, embraced Say's law, making it unassailable doctrine until the 1930s and the Great Depression. The debacle of the 1930s nonetheless did not preclude a rebirth of Say's law as supply-side economics during the Reagan administration. Its fragile logic is quite irrelevant; what is critical is its moral defense of the rich. And, so it came to pass by the early 1980s, beyond ordinary reason, a popular but flawed understanding of what Adam Smith meant was diminished to the wearing of the Adam Smith necktie (filled with little cameos of Smith's profile) out of devotion only to free markets and to remarkably limited government. Smith, a lecturer on Moral Philosophy at Glasgow, would have rejected both out of four-in-hand. Still, according to the wearers of the Adam Smith necktie, government is the problem; the market is the solution. During the early Reagan presidential years, the supply-siders believed tax cuts to be the route to diminished government. In this way, the supply-siders rejected the Keynesians and the inherent instability they attribute to capitalism. Amazingly, supply-side economics became part of the agenda of the New Democrats and Bill Clinton and was more hypocritically embraced by the George W. Bush administration.

The Rejected Keynesian Perspective

A contrary view of the connection or not between personal savings and real business investment emanates from John Maynard Keynes, the economist initially embraced but soon rejected by Alan Greenspan. As noted, Ayn Rand and Arthur Burns had a lot to do with Greenspan's conversion to conservative business fundamentalism. To Keynes, of course, is attributed a contrary notion about unemployment—that great fluctuations in output and employment are consequences of capitalism's excesses. Keynes also stands J. B. Say on his head by suggesting that real business investment, driven mostly by sales to consumers, decides how much income a nation enjoys, out of which to have more real saving. A comparable Keynes' law would say that business investment causes saving. What greatly alienated Greenspan and other business conservatives from Keynesianism is what comes next: When business investment is too small, as during the Great Depression, government alone is capable of investing enough in public works to smooth the business cycle and maintain or restore full employment.

Quite possibly they—Adam Smith, J. B. Say, John Maynard Keynes, and Alan Greenspan—are all wrong, an issue to which we will return. For now we concede that the great contest in U.S. economic policy still springs from the ideas attributed to two intellectual giants—Adam Smith and Maynard Keynes. Will the world of public opinion now place Alan Greenspan alongside these two masters? Is there more to the Greenspan Standard and central banking than the genius of Adam Smith and J. B. Say? As it turns out, there is a great deal more and a great deal less.

3

WHEN MARKETS HAVE FAILED, GREENSPAN HAS BEEN ON THE SCENE

Markets collapsing are nothing new; what is new is a laissez-faire central bank creating the conditions that—without proper regulation—leads to market failures. After all, Alan Greenspan as well as Fed heads before and surely after him, express the profound Smithian belief that markets operate perfectly if left alone. Herein lays a paradox or a pair of something. First, before and after becoming a legendary central banker, Alan Greenspan has been a global leader in the creation of financial and economic crises. Second, during his many terms as Fed chairman, the securities market players have reacted quickly and decisively to even modest movements in closely watched economic and financial omens while hanging on every word he utters. Ironically, the worst terror is a crash in the market individuals happen to be.

When God Crashes

All of which leads to a different way of viewing financial markets; this other road not taken by financial experts may help to explain why Alan Greenspan has been present at many failures of otherwise "perfect" markets. Risk has a way of making itself obvious at once to many players. Fear is contagious and quickly infects virtually everyone until crowd psychology drives asset values away from their fundamental or true economic values, much as the history of manias suggests. Speculative bubbles, a product of crowd euphoria, move asset prices from their conventionally expected values. Selecting from two brands of behavior—collective rationality or irrationality—we can plunk for those who say that crashes can't happen, or we can observe wildly gyrating securities prices, minute-by-minute, on CNBC.

The lack of liquidity is the most severe problem with a system wide failure. *Liquidity* is the measure of the quickness with which we can turn an asset into cash without incurring great costs. A market having many buyers and sellers exhibits liquidity, but even the gigantic U.S. bond market is not immune to a liquidity crisis. When insufficient buyers exist, investment bankers on Wall Street are not going to agree to underwrite even new U.S. Treasuries. An unopened bond market ends liquidity as the bond holders know it. When the system fails, diversification such as holding corporate bonds in several different industries loses whatever powers it might have had. Even if The Market *is* God, the financial wealth holders do not like to see God crash.

The Crash of Milken's Junk Bond Market

The worst-case scenario comes out of a market whose liquidity depends upon the sales ability and manipulation of one or a few persons, whether they be market players or persuasive central bankers. The story of the Milken market illustrates both cases because of not only Alan Greenspan's private and public roles, but also of its snow-balling effects on the credit and stock markets.

Michael Milken, the junk-bond king at Drexel Burnham Lambert, fueled the 1980s leveraged buyout boom. The central idea behind junk-funded buyouts or takeovers is quite simple. First, the takeover artist borrows cash by issuing newly-minted high-yielding (junk) bonds in a market created—in this event, by Milken. Then, the artist pounces on the low-priced stock of a troubled corporation, buys a controlling interest with the cash, lays off a quarter of its labor force, closes a fifth of the company's "stores," generates profits by working fewer workers longer hours, sells the corporation at a huge personal profit, and pays high interest to the junk bond holders until the debt is retired. As others have moved into takeovers, they use the same business model.

Although Michael Milken became fabulously wealthy, in March 1989 authorities indicted him on ninety-eight counts of securities' violations, including racketeering charges. Soon, the Securities and

Exchange Commission (SEC) virtually took over Drexel, which agreed to pay Milken $70 million for his equity in the firm. After plea-bargaining and fingering arbitrager Ivan Boesky, Milken began a 22-month prison term. Without his genius sales ability, however, Drexel could not pedal the junk bonds of Milken's clients. Instead the firm ended up having to buy the junk paper out of its own capital (called proprietary trading), leaving Drexel with a giant portfolio of its own junk. A member of the Forbes 400 since 1986, Michael held $1 billion in net worth in 2004, his brother, $800 million.

Before, when Drexel's large bond issuers had threatened default, Milken had restructured the debt, usually with even more leverage, resembling nothing so much as a pyramid scheme. The remaining sales force at Drexel, however, was unable to "roll over" weak debt into new junk bonds. Besides, Drexel's big clients such as Columbia Savings and Loan and Executive Life, had filled their cupboards with junk bonds and could not ingest more. The companies built on the piles of junk paper began to crumble. Integrated Resources and the giant retailer Campeau Corporation collapsed into bankruptcy. Columbia and Executive Life eventually joined the crowd.

Alan Greenspan and Junk Bonds Contribute to the Savings & Loan Failures

Milken's junk bonds and even Alan Greenspan's Wall Street consultancy played pivotal roles in the monumental collapse of the Savings & Loan industry as well as the related stock market debacles. In the prototypical case, the notorious Lincoln Savings & Loan not only engaged in outright thievery, but its trading in junk bonds and foreign currencies contributed to an expensive failure. Heavily involved with junk bond king Milken and Drexel Burnham, Charles Keating transformed Lincoln from a home mortgage lender to an Arizona land developer, junk bond lender, and player in the takeover market.

The potential for financial disaster from speculation led the Federal Home Loan Bank, a government supervisory agency and lender to the S & Ls, to impose a ten percent limitation on such non-mortgage business. Greenspan, between government positions at the time, had ended his time as head of President Reagan's Council of Economic Advisers, and had returned to his lucrative position as a private consultant. He wrote a laudatory and possibly false letter February 13, 1985 for Keating supporting his application for exemption from the ten percent rule. In his letter to the Federal Home Loan Bank of San Francisco, Greenspan described Lincoln as "an association that has, through its skill and expertise, transformed itself into a financially strong institution that presents no foreseeable risk to the Federal Savings & Loan Corporation," the depository insurance agency for the industry. After receiving $40,000 for writing the letter, Greenspan also endorsed the soundness of Keating's use of insured deposits to buy junk bonds from Michael Milken.

Unfortunately, by the end of 1987 and only a few months after Greenspan had been appointed head of the Fed, Lincoln's interest-bearing liabilities exceeded its interest-bearing assets by more than $1 *billion*. Lincoln's *negative net worth* doubled during the next year. Keating, if not Greenspan, knew that he was working Jessie James's territory. Though Keating controlled Lincoln Savings & Loan, he refused to be an officer or director. Asked why, his reply was that he "did not want to go to jail." In this way junk bonds, though still flying high, not only led to the collapse of an entire industry, but to great losses by senior pensioners and a bailout by taxpayers. Alan Greenspan's remarkable record of mistakes costly to ordinary Americans was gaining momentum.

The Stock Market Crash of 1987

One of the greatest market failures in world history came between Greenspan's new appointment and the collapse of Lincoln S & L. The timing, while ironic, is not entirely coincidental. On August 3, 1987, the U.S. Senate had confirmed Dr. Greenspan as chairman of the Reserve. On Monday, October 19, 1987, the Dow plunged 508 points, losing more than a fifth of its value and nearly $1 trillion in wealth in one day. It was the largest percentage loss ever in one day, eclipsing the worst days of the 1929 crash. Alan had chaired his first Federal Open Market Committee (FOMC) meeting exactly two months earlier. In what became a regular pattern before Greenspan took charge of FOMC meetings, the committee members spent several hours in a roundtable discussion at, ironically, too, a huge 27-foot-long *oval* table. Then, in his trademark understated tone, Greenspan began to speak.

"We spent all morning, and no one even mentioned the stock market, which I find interesting in itself." According to Bob Woodward's account, in which Greenspan is the obvious source of what he was "intending" at the time, "He meant to convey something significantly stronger: For God's sake, he was trying to tell them, …There was a whole other world out there—a world that included the stock market, which had run up thirty percent since the beginning of the year." Corporate takeovers and speculation had Wall Street in a grip that it was losing. In the re-telling of this story to Bob Woodward, Alan had it all figured out; the economy was "over-heated."

Since the FOMC was not scheduled to meet until late September, Greenspan's only option was to increase the discount rate, the interest rate that the Fed charges depository institutions for loans. At the time, changes in the discount rate were publicly announced and changes in the fed funds rate target were not. By talking with each Governor in private, Alan was able to convince them to support a discount rate increase. This too became a pattern in Greenspan's getting what he wanted. Conveniently, when the Board of Governors met for a vote, two were out of town while one vacancy remained on the seven-member board, so only four voting members were present, voting "unanimously" to raise the discount rate a half percentage point to six percent. The subsequent press release announced the rate hike as necessary to fight "potential" inflation. According to Woodward's *anonymous* source, "Greenspan felt that it was crucial to maintain both the Fed's credibility and his own credibility as an inflation fighter." The immediate stock market reaction was negative, but at the end of the day the Dow Jones was down only 38 points.

Although stock prices remained high, the savings & loan crisis to which Greenspan had earlier contributed came up to bite him from behind. Over the weekend of October 17–18, Manuel Johnson, the vice chairman of the Board of Governors, was trying to find a buyer for the American Savings & Loan Association, then the largest savings & loan in the U.S. This financial firm had secretly informed the Reserve that they were going to announce bankruptcy on Monday unless someone bailed them out. The "thrift's" problem was pretty much the same as Lincoln S & L's; American Savings had too big a portfolio of junk bonds. Worse, thanks to Greenspan's hiking of the discount rate, interest rates had taken another upward leap despite no sign of inflation on the horizon. Since the price of bonds move the opposite direction as interest rates, the value of the bonds of both American Savings and Lincoln sunk until both thrifts were broke. The entire S & L industry was about to go bust.

Even the resourceful Johnson, a disciplined ex-Marine, could not find a buyer for American Savings. On Black Monday, October 19, it did go bust, and the stock market crashed. The ball was back in Johnson's court as the official crisis manager at the Federal Reserve in Washington, D.C.: Greenspan was in Dallas to give a speech that he later had to be convinced he should cancel and fly back to the capital. Meantime, Johnson reviewed the possible actions with the Fed's senior staff. Among the possibilities were open market buying of bonds to keep money flowing and short-term interest rates from rising further, organizing stock purchases by major securities firms, and targeted Fed lending specifically designed to support stock prices. An ambiguous provision of the Federal Reserve Act would allow the Fed, with the agreement of five of the seven members of its board to make loans to brokerage houses and other non-banks. Later, Greenspan expressed a willingness to make illegal deals, such as lending money only to those institutions that agreed to do what the Fed wanted them to do.

E. Gerald Corrigan, a profane and smart Irishman, was then the outspoken president of the Federal Reserve Bank of New York on the edge of Wall Street in every respect. As have all New York Fed presidents, Corrigan had close ties with the CEOs of the city's commercial banks such as Citibank, the investment banking firms such as Goldman Sachs, and the stock brokerage houses such as Merrill Lynch. Any payments or receipts delays among these financial giants would trigger a downward cascade of liquidity into illiquidity. The financial system would either seize-up or explode.

Corrigan convinced Greenspan to issue a one-sentence statement before the financial markets opened on Tuesday. They agreed to: "The Federal Reserve, consistent with its responsibilities as the nation's central bank, affirmed today its readiness to serve as a source of liquidity to support the economic and financial system."

Corrigan convinced Greenspan to back this statement up with actions that Corrigan himself would take. Meanwhile the stock market was near collapse as well as the Chicago options exchange. Options are low-priced contracts to buy or sell a specified number of shares of a stock at a future date. Stock in IBM, the bluest of the Blue Chips, stopped trading because all the trading orders were to sell. Corrigan meanwhile convinced major banks and brokerage firms to make payments good even if a firm's credit was in doubt. Corrigan and Johnson also devised a contingency plan: The Fed would directly guarantee payments between brokerage firms as well as continuing to lend funds to the private banks. The plan was kept secret because banks and brokerage houses otherwise would take the guarantees and run instead of using their own money.

Tuesday afternoon the stock market rallied on the strength of the then largest rally in the history of the Major Market Index futures market. No one claims to know why, and Corrigan didn't want to know because several firms and individuals might have illegally manipulated the market. Worse, someone in the U.S. Treasury or the Fed might have quietly approved the actions. One known illegal action was taken on Thursday after the president of the Chicago Fed called to say that First Options, a subsidiary of Continental Illinois, and a bank too large to fail, was broke and could no long issue new loans to the options market. At the time, the Fed, as the regulator of commercial banks, maintained a firewall between Continental's depositor's funds and such trading subsidiaries as First Options. Yet Continental sought relief from the firewall to keep First Options from going under. Johnson knew that the failure of giant First Options would send the options market into a tailspin and possibly trigger another stock market plunge.

"Let them do it," Johnson said. "Don't block it. Let the money go. We'll clean this up later."

According to Bob Woodward, "Greenspan just nodded."

Ending George H.W. Bush's Political Career;
Bailing Out Citibank and the Global Financial System

The Federal Open Market Committee was quite divided during 1988 and 1989. As Greenspan took tighter control of the Committee, he also moved toward a much tighter monetary policy, fearing that inflation had become a serious problem. It was an awkward time politically because Ronald Reagan would soon be leaving town and George H.W. Bush would be running for president. The increases in the fed funds rate were dramatic. Eventually, Greenspan's tightening would lead to a sharp economic recession and, later, contribute greatly to the defeat of Bush I in his run for a second term—this despite a slow reversal to lower interest rates going into the campaign for a second Bush term, with Greenspan clearly concerned about his re-appointment. Meanwhile, there would be other causalities (besides those of the first Gulf War).

The stock market turmoil continued even as financial fragility came full circle. The entire Milken market pyramid collapsed with the October 1989 "mini-crash" of the U.S. stock market close on the heels of the 1987 crash. Takeover stocks "backed" by junk bonds led the October 13, 1989 190-point market plunge, then the second-greatest points drop in its history. Greenspan said nothing but vice chairman Manuel Johnson told reporters that the Fed was ready to pump liquidity into the system, just as it had after the 1987 crash. This "independent" move by Johnson angered Greenspan for several reasons, not the least of which was the vice chairman's "insubordination." (An ex-Marine should have known better.) The whole junk bond market collapsed as junk-bond issuers began to default on their obligations. As a result, junk bonds were yielding a negative eleven point two percent by 1990.

As Greenspan elevated short-term interest rates to fight inflation, long-term interest rates were signaling recession. The two sets of rates began to converge, eventually approaching an "inversion." Normally, long-term rates are higher than short-term rates because there is more risk to lending money for longer periods requiring a risk premium. (A somewhat similar situation would develop in spring 2005, to which we later turn.) Banks make profits by borrowing short-term and lending long-term; they run into a profits squeeze when interest rates converge. By November 1990 Greenspan was facing a banking crisis not only because of the convergence of rates (his doing) but the failure of bank real estate loans in Latin America and elsewhere (the private banks doing).

As usual, the President of the Fed Bank of New York was closest to the situation. Gerald Corrigan knew that the biggest bank in the world, Citibank (now Citigroup), was the closest to financial collapse. It was insolvent. Its collapse—and this is beginning to sound familiar—would endanger the global financial system. As Bob Woodward reports, "Corrigan arranged a come-to-Jesus meeting with [Citibank head John] Reed and informed Greenspan of his plan," to which Greenspan gave, as usual, his "tacit approval."

Corrigan told Reed that Citi needed $5 billion in new capital within six months. Who better than a prince, Prince Alwaleed bin Talal, a young Saudi Arabian of extreme wealth, to supply such a princely sum? In a secret meeting in Saudi Arabia, Corrigan laid out the rules to Prince Talal. The Prince already owned a lot of Citi stock and was willing to invest another $1.2 billion, giving him about fourteen percent ownership of Citibank as the largest single shareholder. With this and a new management plan from John Reed, Citibank needed only one more small favor. Greenspan and Corrigan knew that a lower short-term fed funds rate (lowering Citibank and other banks' prime rate and other rates) would be required, creating a profit-assured spread against long-term rates. Greenspan came through.

A Legend is Born Amidst the Chaos

Thus began the Greenspan legend as the greatest central banker on the planet. Wall Street and neoconservative politicians gave him the credit for "saving capitalism." But, even in the telling by Bob Woodward, Johnson and Corrigan are the heroes; Greenspan seemed to be putting himself in a position of deniability if the stock market did not turn around in 1987 and deniability if anything went wrong with the Saudi-Citibank deal. He never agreed on paper to anything (including the illegalities); Johnson and Corrigan had to interpret the nods of his head. Besides, the combination of Greenspan's private endorsement of junk bonds and his private and public cheer-leading for deregulation of the S & Ls and commercial banks helped to create the financial fragility that needed only his singular finger on the discount rate trigger to take down the stock market in 1987, fed funds increases to take it down in 1989, as well as Citibank thereafter. Even the reason he gave for the discount rate and fed funds rate increases—to fight inflation—were false in the first instance and wrong in the second. These actions on behalf of Wall Street nonetheless made Greenspan a legend in his spare time.

What Greenspan did became his model for "risk management" during his many terms. Oddly, financial markets in the post-WWII era had not required much risk management when they had been severely regulated and when the marginal tax rates of the very rich had been high. The financial crises still to come were the product of the market fundamentalism that had led to the Milken junk bond market, the S & L thefts, the crash of 1987, the mini-crash of 1989, and the Citibank crisis. Alan Greenspan contributed mightily to them all, but he had help from others. Critical to his legendary status, Wall Street gave him credit for preserving its way of life.

4

THE INDEPENDENCE OF
ALAN GREENSPAN AND THE
FEDERAL RESERVE SYSTEM

*"Is the market irrational?" asked Helen Thomas, a veteran reporter
from United Press International. "Do you stick by your previous
statements on the stock market?"*
"You surely don't want me to answer that," Greenspan replied.
"Yes, I do."
"You do?" he asked. "Well, I don't think I will."

An exchange at the White House upon the announcement of the
re-nomination of Alan Greenspan as chairman of the
Federal Reserve System, January 4, 2000.

The question naturally arises: Can the wizard of money remain hidden
behind the curtain while influencing every market in the world? Alan
Greenspan's last appearance on a talk or interview show where he might
be subjected to journalistic cross-examination was Sunday, October 4,
1987, shortly after his initial appointment as head of the Fed. He was
on *This Week with David Brinkley* trying desperately to avoid clarity.
There are no signs of inflation picking up but those signs might be
just around the corner. The Reserve might have to raise the fed funds
rate, but it might not. Greenspan thereafter went off the television
talk show circuit. Later, when asked at a party how he was, Greenspan
joked, "I'm not allowed to say." Soon, Greenspan learned how to give
speeches devoid of any specific meaning. He has secrets he intends not
to share; despite this intent, wealth holders around the world hang on
his every word. Ironical, isn't it?

Helen Thomas, now retired, was once a thorn in the side of many a president of the United States. It would be difficult, however, to document occasions in which a president refused to answer a question, though many on many occasions have given an answer to a different question. A few have given answers that were incomprehensible, seldom by intent. Alan Greenspan, as head of the Fed, always has reserved the right *not* to answer questions, as well as the right of first confusion. He is the master of obscurity even when speaking of transparency, thereby furthering the cult of secrecy of the central bank: Greenspan has added twists and turns to this independence so as to make it his own. As part of his legacy, transparency manifested as invisibility will endure.

Greenspan's arrogance is subdued. When testifying before Congress, he conceals from only the most sophisticated observer, his impatience with members of inferior intelligence or knowledge of arcane financial transactions or accounting. In the end he is pleased because he has successfully revealed nothing, or nothing that they would understand until it is too late.

While the maestro may be the master, the general character of the Fed, like most central banks in the industrialized world, is resistant to change. The "political independence" of the Reserve is no small thing. Its basic premise is so obvious as to be embarrassing: the general public cannot be trusted, whereas this "Supreme Court of Finance" is regally above and beyond the influence of the carping citizen. Alan Greenspan and other Fed officials can exert their power over financial markets and, more generally, the economy with no need to take account of the various special interest groups—or, in truth, the general public.

The U.S. Supreme Court, also the head the judiciary branch of government, is "independent" of the White House and of the Congress. Why, then, should anyone wring hands, gnash teeth or furrow brow about the independence of the Fed. First, the Federal Reserve System is *not* constitutionally a fourth branch of government. This condition holds for other central banks around the world. Second, the Reserve is no ordinary enterprise, for it has enormous powers to be exercised across the national economy and even globally. Hence, it is in the rather anomalous position of having powers that affect, directly and indirectly, everyone in the country and many abroad with no clearly defined responsibilities to constitutional government.

That a central banker such as Alan Greenspan has enormous powers is itself of concern, but, as with Mr. Greenspan, the central defense of independence from other parts of government is the necessity of avoiding political infectivity. Greenspan and the Fed, generally, have claimed to be studiously "nonpolitical." Alan Greenspan's political activism, coming as it does from a strong Randian and neoconservative ideological base, is sufficient reason to ask whether the central bank's Olympian independence has any place in a democratic society. But, it is not the only reason.

OLIPHANT © (2002) UNIVERSAL PRESS SYNDICATE. Reprinted with permission. All rights reserved.

The Misplaced Populist's Origins of the Fed

Oddly, misplaced populist sentiment forged the Federal Reserve Act of 1913 that established the Reserve. Each of the seven members of the

Federal Reserve Board, the ruling body of the Federal Reserve System, is to be appointed for one fourteen-year term, a compromise with the lifelong appointments of Supreme Court Judges. By law, the appointments must yield a "fair representation of the financial, agricultural, industrial, and commercial interests and geographical divisions for the country," and no two Governors may come from the same of twelve Federal Reserve Districts. The Governors' appointments are staggered so that one term expires on January 31 of each even-numbered year.

The President of the United States, elected for a four-year term by commoners, can probably appoint a few new members to the Fed's Board of Governors, but not a controlling majority, nor members exclusively of the President's choosing. Since the Chairman of the Board is named by the President from among the Governors and confirmed by the Senate for a term of four years, and since no Governor can be "removed from office for their policy views," an incoming president is stuck with the current chair of the Board unless their terms of office coincide.

These laws and the pontifical formalities of their discharge have chiseled purity into the marbled walls of the Board's regal headquarters in Washington D.C. The high purpose of the Fed was the same as for the Supremes; purification would come though "independence" from unwashed politicos. These formal edicts not only still stand, they have become sacred as Mr. Greenspan has approached sainthood. As with so much of biblical magnitude, these noble-sounding edicts are now irrelevant—made irrelevant by Mr. Greenspan's longevity in politics, his political acumen, his institutionally-enhanced powers, as well as the Fed's institutional memory in apparent perpetuity. Knowing this, "fair representation" and the highly-touted "political independence" of the Reserve on a late-night David Letterman show qualify for nine and ten on a comical list of central bank characteristics.

But, there is more, much more. The powers of Mr. Greenspan and other Fed chairmen are not exercised in a vacuum, despite so many of their speeches being empty of content. The potentially more damaging features of the Fed do not appear in formal declarations and are not even publicized. In conformity with well-meaning populism compromised by financial interests, the Reserve was not initially set up as a centralized public bank (unlike the others in the industrialized world). Geographic diversity was designed to diffuse the Reserve's power. Moreover, the Reserve, by a conception by now considered immaculate by its Wall Street laity, would be owned privately by bankers. The Federal Reserve became that great oxymoron of public policy, a *quasi*-public institution. Privatization came effortlessly, long before such matters were dictated by libertarians.

The Act establishing the Federal Reserve System in 1913 was paved, not with gold, but with good intentions. Under the Gold Standard that spanned much of the nineteenth century, the growth in the supply of money had depended on the vagaries of gold and silver mining. More often than not, illiquidity in private banks led to what then were quaintly called "panics" followed by "depressions." The United States experienced frequent financial panics in which bank reserves were inadequate to cover sudden withdrawals of deposits. In an irony now fully appreciated, the Fed was mandated to counter the terrible consequences of the Gold Standard. The original purposes of the Fed, as expressed by its founding fathers, were "to give the country an elastic currency, to provide facilities for discounting commercial paper, and to improve the supervision of banking." By "elastic currency" they meant money and credit supplies responsive to the needs of a growing nation, what the Gold Standard was not providing.

The Early and Massive Mistakes by the Fed

There have been, as ever, unintended consequences. The most significant was the Federal Reserve System's failure to act as lender of last resort to a collapsing banking system during the early 1930s. The reason for the Reserve's miss-step provides an important lesson lost long ago on Ayn Rand, Mr. Greenspan and neoconservatives; the Fed's mistakes then came from its privatization. The way that the twelve Fed banks were to conduct their "quasi-private" business guaranteed their failure to stabilize the economy in the 1930s.

The Fed banks bought the short-term debt notes that private banks created when they lent to business places and to farmers. To "discount" this commercial paper each of the twelve Reserve banks had, and still have, a discount window. When the bankers were naughty, instead of going to confession, they went to the discount window, which was supposed to be a window of opportunity. Since the cash received by the private banks was less than the face value of the notes, the discount rate provided interest to the Reserve Banks. If business was bad and private bankers could not find takers for loans, the Federal Reserve banks refused to lend money to the private bankers. They essentially slammed shut the discount window. When business was good and private bankers had many takers for loans, the Reserve banks lent like crazy. The discount window was opened wide. That is, the Federal Reserve banks behaved just like the private banks, even to the point of each Fed bank deciding its own discount rate and its own ease or tightness in lending. By doing what the private bankers were doing—lending less to the private bankers in bad times meant that the bankers would be less able to lend to homeowners and businesses in bad times—the Fed banks contributed to the plunge in economic activity that set off the Great Depression. Currency ended up being no more "elastic" than steel balls dropped from the leaning tower of Pisa.

A Centralized Fed Turns Its Guns on Real and Imaginary Inflation

The massive failure of the Fed to conduct a policy in the public's interest led to reform legislation in 1935 that centralized power and budget-setting in the Federal Reserve Board and the Federal Open Market Committee (FOMC). The FOMC, led by its collective nose by Alan Greenspan and Fed chairs before and henceforth, is comprised of the seven Governors plus five Federal Reserve Bank presidents on a rotating basis, excepting the president of the New York Federal Reserve Bank, who is a permanent member. The FOMC sets the fed funds rate target and thus short-term interest rates in the United States. Since the chair of the FOMC is the chair of the Board of Governors, Alan Greenspan, prior chairmen, and future chairs decide short-term interest rates.

Bankers do not like inflation because it erodes the value of their currency, which, of course, is "money in the bank." Their concern is not directly with goods prices—that $1000 suits begin to cost $1100 or ten percent more—but with the decline in the value of money. Steel makers feel the same way about the price of steel. Purchasing power is decreased by inflation in goods prices; they are two ends of a teeter-totter. Private lenders of money do not want to be repaid in dollars that are worth less (goods being priced higher). The Fed, still tethered to private commercial bankers, sensed inflation was just around the corner during an economic recovery underway in 1937. The now centralized Fed fired its twelve guns in unison, reduced liquid assets in the private banking system, allowed interest rates to rise, and created a business recession in the midst of a business recession. The Fed is responsible for making the 1930s depression the *Great* Depression.

Like most central banks, the Federal Reserve became not just the enemy of inflation, but the foe of imaginary inflation. A second world war not only followed the Great Depression but ended it by employing an entire generation of males (and some females). The most watched over ideas, even the fear of politicians or of goods inflation, often are set aside during wartime. The independence of the Fed was ceded to the U.S. Treasury to finance WWII at low interest rates. The Treasury-Fed accord of 1951 withdrew this financing responsibility, and by 1956 President Eisenhower was speaking of Fed independence in terms that delighted conservative bankers: "The Federal Reserve is set up as a separate agency of Government. It is not under the authority of the President, and I . . . believe it would be a mistake to make it responsible to the political head of state." The General who had led the invasion of Normandy had just surrendered the White House to the Reserve. And, just as there was once a second pope in Avignon, the spirited independence of the Fed once ceded to the U.S. Treasury, was renounced, and, once again, there was only one "Pope of Wall Street," as Greenspan has often been called.

Today, the President of the United States and the public acquiesce in monetary management without representation. In late 1996 Chairman Greenspan tied the necessity of Americans "grudging acceptance of the degree of independence afforded our institutions [the Fed]" to the fight against goods inflation:

> It is generally recognized and appreciated that if the Federal Reserve's monetary policy decisions were subject to

Congressional or Presidential override, short-term political forces would dominate. The clear political preference for lower interest rates would unleash inflationary forces, inflicting severe damage on our economy.

OLIPHANT © (1996) UNIVERSAL PRESS SYNIDICATE. Reprinted with permission. All rights reserved.

This great fear of goods inflation did subside for a time after the Internet and tech crash at the turn of this century. Thereafter 9-11 visited the U.S. and much more. Deflation or falling goods prices, in part the by-product of Alan Greenspan's fight against inflation, became a serious concern. He never expressed a wish for congressional or presidential preference for politically motivated lower interest rates. Luckily, by spring 2005 the ghost of goods inflation was again sighted by Dr. Greenspan. We have come full circle among a great number of circles, most of which will be unwound in the next pages.

The Pursuit of Unemployment

What, we might ask, of unemployment? In the beginning there were no Fed instructions to end inflation or for maximizing employment. More recently, the Board of Governors of the Federal Reserve has recognized broader responsibilities to "counteract inflationary movements and to share in creating conditions favorable to sustained high employment, stable values, growth of the country, and a rising level of consumption." This proclamation, though sounding purposeful and good for all Americans, signifies nothing. "High employment" has been defined as the level at which goods inflation will remain zero.

The Reserve's mission has never been allied with the interests of working people or those otherwise poor, during the past quarter century. For ordinary workers the conduct of monetary policy is religion without the sacraments. They have only their own faith to keep. The members of the Reserve's board and its twelve bank presidents have generally served the financial community, its laity. No conspiracy exists; the Federal Reserve no longer is *expected* to serve any other constituency.

5

FEDSPEAK AND THE INNOCENT HYPOCRISY OF INDEPENDENCE

Risk takers have been encouraged by a perceived increase in economic stability to reach out to more distant time horizons. But long periods of relative stability often engender unrealistic expectations of its permanence and, at times, may lead to financial excess and economic stress.

Alan Greenspan, from testimony before the Financial Services Committee, U.S. House of Representatives, July 20, 2005. It was 35th appearance, but probably no representative knew what the maestro meant; namely, a sudden shift in perceptions of the economy could send interest rates on bonds abruptly soaring, squeezing homeowners who have bought pricey homes with adjustable-rate mortgages.

The independence of the Fed may have been born of innocence, but, under Alan Greenspan's stewardship, has achieved hypocrisy in its maturity. While the founders' intent was noble, an institution established as having responsibilities and intelligence beyond reproach is seldom entirely devoid of hypocrisy. In this regard the Fed's independence, like Alan Greenspan's, has always been less than pure. While the chairman has demanded that the Federal Reserve System be entirely independent, this high-minded principle has not prevented Mr. Greenspan from pursuing his personal policy preferences in the White House, the Congress and elsewhere.

The Institutional Hypocrisy

For now, let us consider the institutional hypocrisy, and how it remains an integral part of the independence of the Reserve. As Yogi Berra might say, "the Fed has many features that wouldn't be secrets if people knew about them." Few Americans know that private commercial bankers own shares in the Federal Reserve Banks, or that a small coterie of private investment bankers have intimate ties to the Federal Open Market Committee (FOMC). Once we know what to look for, we can find this information on the Federal Reserve System website (*www.federalreserve.gov*). These little central bank characteristics are only sufficient to be called innocent hypocrisy or even "innocent fraud," to use John Kenneth Galbraith's term. Hypocrisy does not prevent the Federal Reserve System from cultivating its own version of the truth, which benefits its own constituency and thus engenders no guilt. It is innocent hypocrisy.

Beyond the secrets people don't know about because they misjudge the Fed's guiltless powers, there are "true secrets." During financial crises, what transpires among these powerful but private financial denizens remain mostly unknown. Since we are accustomed to clandestine meetings between the White House and the Central Intelligence Agency (CIA), between Deep Throat and Woodstein (Woodward and Bernstein), the secrecy could be considered of small concern. When we are told that money is too complicated and mysterious to understand, that is another matter. Federal Reserve operations made impenetrable through the cultivation of the mystique of money serves only a small class of individuals and financial firms. They are in on the deals and the actions of the Fed; ordinary citizens are easily deceived because they do not have a large enough immediate and direct stake in outcomes. In four words, most people are *not financial wealth holders*. The Reserve pretends to "benefit" all households, but the typical citizen is not a member of the financial team. Kept off the infield and not even allowed in the ball park makes the Fed's self-aggrandizing judgment self-fulfilling.

As with the hand signals between a Red Sox pitcher and his catcher, a secret language is power and monetary policy is a private affair conducted behind closed gates. Afterward, even when the gates are thrown open, very little is revealed. Sometimes there is some connection between the speeches and testimony of Fed officials and their curve balls, but we usually don't know what it is, until afterwards—at home plate. The typical family has just lost half its retirement wealth, though it is a small stake, while the individuals and firms with the *real* wealth have been bailed out in secret meetings. Again, all of this would be much more acceptable if citizens had not been told that it can't be any of their business because they would never really understand money, having so little of it themselves.

Greenspan: The Master of Fedspeak

A few weeks before the testimony in the above epigram, I recall watching Alan Greenspan testify before the Joint Economic Committee of Congress. He was "explaining," among other things, why, despite eight successive increases in the fed funds rate, long-term interest rates had fallen below key short-term rates. Like many academic economists, Greenspan is a master with numbers. Some perky members asked really good questions, such as, "Mr. Greenspan, sir, does the Federal Reserve have the tools to end the apparent bubble in housing prices?" But, after Greenspan had mentioned five or six different indexes, their rates of change, and the rates of change in their rates of change, the eyes of even the most alert congressperson glazed over. Then, when Greenspan gave, in detail, three different "hypotheses" for an interest-rate "conundrum" (mortgage rates falling as shorter rates were rising), even the eyes of the most sympathetic questioners shifted toward the exits. What Greenspan did may have been unintentional, but it served his purposes. I, a Ph.D. economist and once employed by the Federal Reserve Bank of St. Louis (with a lowly Masters degree), knew that Dr. Greenspan had given at least two contradictory answers for each question that he answered. In a world of two-handed economists ("on the other hand"), Greenspan is an octopus. Still, his words were, as ever, carefully chosen.

One congressman was particularly irritated and suggested something like, "Those fed funds rate decreases have substituted a housing bubble for a stock market bubble." Then, he asked, "If you had it to do again, would you still have lowered the fed funds rate to only one percent?" "Given what we know now," Greenspan "believed that the FOMC made the right decisions." When the head of the Fed speaks, especially when it has been Greenspan, it is *ex cathedra*. Infallibility comes to mind, only to soon be erased. Later in the hearings, when asked what the "real" fed funds rate (the money rate adjusted for goods inflation) *should* be, Greenspan said that he didn't know and even if he did, it would be of no use because he wouldn't know what to do since Fed actions would change it. I thought I heard several members of congress slump to the floor.

Greenspan, like his predecessors, used to have much to say about the money supply until sometime in 1998, very little thereafter. He frequently changed his definition of "money supply" since the Reserve publishes M1, M2, and then M3. These money supplies become larger though less liquid (or more distant from cash) as they approach M, which includes even institutional time deposits. The most liquid of the Ms is M1 which *includes* cash. Though Greenspan once gave Congress money supply "targets," they were sufficiently wide to be nearly meaningless. Besides, when the Reserve failed to hit even a broad target, Greenspan then redefined it. To the Congress and to the White House, Alan Greenspan himself became a moving target. He had admitted by omission in 1998 that the Fed had been targeting the fed funds rate as its sole policy tool for several years; the various money supplies just went along for the ride.

What the Fed will do in the near or far future is a guessing game. Ironically, the wizard of money has demanded that banks in Southeastern Asia be more "transparent." Whether we define transparency as clarity or something else, Greenspan's confusing congressional testimony has left understanding as mere dust on the floor of the Congress. Beginning informally in 1994 and formally in February 1995, the Fed adopted the practice of announcing policy changes immediately following its FOMC meetings. However, few understand the announcements; they lead to much second or even third and fourth-guessing. An entire industry has evolved around "Fed Watchers," analysts who attempt to translate Fedspeak.

The edited minutes of FOMC meetings are now released after three weeks to provide still more "transparency." The content nonetheless continues to cause guests on CNBC business news to shake their heads and argue about what "Greenspan meant" such as when he refers to long-term interest rates lower than short-term rates as a "conundrum," adding that this might be a "short-term aberration." Synonyms for conundrum include "mystery" and "riddle": while an aberration can be "oddity" or "eccentricity." So, are long term rates below short term rates a mysterious short term oddity or eccentric short term riddle? Alan Greenspan, who adores the transparency that he sees in free markets even when opaqueness prevails, has managed to give transparency a bad name.

Consider a sample of what even well-schooled Fed watchers must decipher from the terse policy statements of the Federal Open Market Committee. After increasing the federal funds rate target to three point two five percent in its June 29–30, 2005 meetings, the FOMC writes:

> The Committee perceives that, with appropriate monetary policy action, the upside and downside risks to the attainment of both sustainable growth and price stability should be kept roughly equal. With underlying inflation expected to be contained, the Committee believes that policy accommodation can be removed at a pace that is likely to be measured. Nonetheless, the Committee will respond to changes in economic prospects as needed to fulfill its obligation to maintain price stability.

The Fed Watchers have to comb every word of the eight pages of minutes to attempt to understand this "transparent" statement. We need to know what the Committee (i.e., Greenspan) means by "sustainable growth" (how fast?), "price stability" (which inflation rate?), "underlying inflation" (not overlying?), and "measured pace" (how fast?). One thing is perfectly clear; the Fed is worried about inflation even though at the time it is not discernable in anything except in the price of crude oil (over which the Fed has no control) and the price of an asset, housing (over which the FOMC claims it wants no control).

Although Greenspan was once a moderate monetarist, he had always been less doctrinaire than Nobelist Milton Friedman, the founder of modern monetarism who for decades claimed that excessive growth in the money supply is the *only* cause of inflation. (He now recants.) Greenspan's pragmatism and experience at the Federal Reserve led him to the belief that only interest rates matter. Besides, the fed funds rate is the only tool that the FOMC can control. He never tells us what the fed funds rate might next be because that would be to give away his greatest source of financial power, except for his power as a financial icon.

TOLES © (2001) The Washington Post. Reprinted with permission of UNIVERSAL PRESS SYNDICATE. All rights reserved.

Money, whether or not it is defined as M2, remains an important dimension of central bank power. Greenspanspeak, the most refined version of Fedspeak, could not be a hypocritical source of Fed independence without the mystery of money—what money is, where it comes from, and where it goes. Since the mystique of money is a useful tool in itself, the Fed has long attempted to cultivate a profound lack of understanding. Alan Greenspan became the master of such mysteries as the creator of a language all his own. He is clear on a few matters: his statements on past policy normally blame economic adversity on forces beyond the Fed's control, while eagerly accepting credit for any good news. Still, there are institutional reasons why the head of the Fed can use Fedspeak as a means to the goal of unaccountability.

Wealth as a Fountainhead of Independence

Like its wealthy constituency, capital gains and interest make the Federal Reserve System self-financing. It earns capital gains and interest on the Fed's vast holdings of U.S. Treasury securities. The Fed's banks might even be more profitable than their private owners. The Federal Open Market Committee has had the power to buy and sell such securities since open market operations were accidentally discovered during the 1920s. The System receives interest and capital gains (and losses) from its vast government securities dealings. It can't lose: when capital gains are down, interest payments are up, and when interest payments are down, capital gains are up. It is an innocent hypocrisy shared with its constituency: This isn't a secret; it's just that almost no one *knows* that the Federal Reserve is self-financing. The Reserve pays its own formidable expenses out of its own formidable earnings.

Not only do these resources insulate the System from congressional budgetary threats, they provide funds sufficient to build new, multi-billion dollar regional banks. Today, its new regional banks are to financial officers what the cathedrals of the Middle Ages were to the abbots, bishops and other prelates. What is not set aside for building monuments to bonds and money is used for high-salaried bank officers, economists, and others. Whatever is left over after "expenses" reverts to the Treasury and, *yes*, helps to reduce deficits or increase surpluses and pay interest to bondholders.

The total income of the twelve Reserve Banks in 2002 was $26.8 billion—or about half the GDP of Ireland—with net expenses of more than $2 billion. Of these expenses, $1.342 billion went into salaries and other personnel expenses. Some $24.5 billion of net income was transferred to the U.S. Treasury as interest on Federal Reserve Notes and $1.1 billion was transferred to "surplus." Among the individual banks, the New York Fed was by far the most expensive to operate, located at it is, on Wall Street. Its salaries were $226.3 million for 3222 employees or $70,326 per employee, well above the legislated minimum wage for ordinary workers that Alan Greenspan has always strongly opposed. Some $313,300 of the total went to the president of the bank, making him a one-percenter. The budget for the Board of Governors is separate from those of the Reserve Banks. In 2002, the total operating expenses of the Board, which is a kind of supra-bank, were $214.2 million with $146 million going into salaries.

The Federal Reserve System is the largest employer of economists in the world, half of whom are at the Board. When this confidential fraternity of economists joins the Reserve, it has been called "taking the veil." Spread around American universities, these economists would fill twenty or more academic departments in major research universities. With so many economist-monks, we might suppose that the Reserve *would be* infallible. Since most ambitious young Ph.D. economists would love to have a well-paid research position at the Fed, those specializing in money, banking and international finance seek these positions. Criticism of the Federal Reserve by economists is as rare as a Buffalo from Wyoming being sighted on Wall Street. After all, we Ph.D.s can become part of the insider world of the Federal Reserve System. We have as much reason to protect and promote the Federal Reserve as the Governors.

Wall Street's Protection

The Reserve's "independence" also is protected by Wall Street, on which the Fed presently is hypocritically dependent. Wall Street has investment banking and other profits directly and indirectly connected to Fed activity. Lightly regulated financial institutions who are allowed to merge willy-nilly will naturally be protective. We need only "follow the money," not only as it flows into Wall Street from special U.S. Treasury and Federal Reserve ties, but as it flows back to the Federal Reserve System. Government securities underwritten at a profit in the private investment banks ultimately become the means to those capital gains and interest income for the Federal Reserve.

The Federal Reserve has the interests of fellow financial institutions at heart. It is quasi-*private*, not quasi-public. The truly private investment and commercial banks depend on the Reserve for their business; the Fed depends on the private investment banks to keep the bond market open for *its* business. Increasingly the financial markets of Wall Street, including the stock markets, depend on the Fed for maintaining as much stability as ever comes to such markets. The public nonetheless is told that the central function of the Fed is to stabilize prices, sustain only sustainable economic growth and promote modest employment. We are never directly told that the Fed's main function is to preserve and protect the interests of wealth holders.

We thus come to one of the dirty secrets of Alan Greenspan and the Reserve. While they are demanding political independence, the Reserve is dependent on private financial institutions, especially those on Wall Street. Thus comprises the innocent institutional hypocrisy of the Federal Reserve. There has never been a great distance between Greenspan and Wall Street. These close ties go a long way toward explaining the evolution of Alan Greenspan as an American icon with more power over financial markets at home and abroad than the President of the United States. We also will consider his hypocrisy of personal interference.

6

WHITE HOUSE DEPENDENCE AND THE HYPOCRISY OF PERSONAL INTERFERENCE

At the president-elect's end of the table, Clinton's face turned red with anger and disbelief. "You mean to tell me that the success of the program and my re-election hinges on the Federal Reserve and a bunch of fucking bond traders?" he responded in a half-whisper. Nods from his end of the table. Not a dissent.

Bob Woodward's account of the initial meeting of Bill Clinton's National Economic Council, January 7, 1993, just 13 days before Clinton's inauguration. See Bob Woodward, *The Agenda: Inside the Clinton White House* (New York: Simon & Schuster, 1994), p. 84.

Greenspan haunts every budget meeting, though his name never comes up directly. Instead, it's always our "credibility" with Wall Street. It is repeatedly said that we must reduce the deficit because Wall Street needs to be reassured, calmed, convinced of our wise intentions.

Robert B. Reich, *Locked in the Cabinet* (New York: Alfred A. Knopf, 1997). Reich was Secretary of Labor during the Clinton administration.

The hypocrisy of an institution fiercely justifying the necessity of its independence while being in the deep pockets of private financial interests is repugnant. It is doubly so because historically it has not always been this way; moreover, it need not be today. Historically, the frequent moaning heard in New York and Washington D.C. is that the two cities have different agendas. Wall Street, they have said, considers the free market to be the litmus test for what is spiritually correct, whereas the White House and the Congress are hell bent on redistributing income and wealth from the rich to the poor. As to the Federal Reserve System, Wall Street has had few complaints; it has had veto power regarding the selection of the Fed chair, going all the way back to the Jimmy Carter years.

The quarrels between Wall Street and the rest of Washington, D.C. officially ended with the beginning of the Clinton Administration. At that time Alan Greenspan and the financial wealth holding class moved Wall Street's agenda into the White House. As President-elect, Bill Clinton virtually turned over White House economic policy to Greenspan, the choice of Wall Street. By mid-April 1993, the administration had embraced the preferences of the financial market players for deficit reduction and free trade. Meanwhile, Clinton, once believed to be America's greatest politician, maneuvered to dilute Greenspan's power. In that endeavor, Clinton failed. In this decisive clash, Greenspan proved that he was the best politician in Washington's history.

Greenspan Presents His Offer Behind Closed Doors

The initial alignment of Clinton and Greenspan seems as unlikely as that of Venus and Mars. After all, Greenspan was a member of a radical right Collective and a close ally of Ayn Rand. In vivid contrast to Greenspan's pedigree, Clinton was a Southern populist who had governed the poor, backward state of Arkansas. He was one of the New Democrats; they were more centrist than the old Democrats, but they nonetheless wished to retain the social programs from Franklin Roosevelt's New Deal. They still believed that the federal government had an important role in maintaining full employment. It was, they believed, the responsibility of the federal government to increase opportunities for the poor, because the rich had the resources to care for themselves. Moreover, Clinton had run for president on a platform of public investment in the infrastructure and in education. By his run for a second term, nonetheless, these issues had long since been abandoned unless "building a bridge to the twenty-first century" is considered a new infrastructure.

Why would the Clinton White House instead agree to an alliance with Alan Greenspan? No doubt deep concerns among those being appointed to positions in the U.S. Treasury contributed to this end. The U.S. Treasury dependence upon the wealth holders to purchase its securities (including foreign bond holders, especially in Japan, Germany and the United Kingdom) had greatly increased as Reagan-Bush I federal deficits mushroomed.

Besides, Clinton was hardly the first President to be undone by the head of the Reserve. Ironically, Alan Greenspan's ineptitude helped defeat Ford and elect the first New Democrat. Later, however, the Reserve got even. Paul Volcker, Greenspan's predecessor, managed to create his first recession in time to inspire the electorate, at long last, to answer Jimmy Carter's plea for self-denial by sacrificing Carter's presidency. We turn now to the travail of the second New Democrat president in his battle of wits with Volcker's successor.

What was once merely an anti-inflationary neurosis at the Federal Reserve crossed an invisible psychological border into a psychosis, culminating in the zero-inflation policy championed by Greenspan, the same Greenspan to later worry about the possibility of *deflation*. A new psychology came forth: Slow economic growth was *good* because it led to higher bond prices and hence a bullish stock market. Interest rates were to be kept low not by an easy money policy but by managing to keep the economy soft. Even the hint of a speed up in economic growth created a chill in the pristine air of the massive, marbled building housing the Federal Reserve Board in Washington, D.C. If necessary, the Reserve would raise short-term interest rates so that longer-term or bond interest rates might fall from a slowing economy. This commanding view is manifestly the ideal financial markets strategy for benefiting the financial wealth holders.

A new revolutionary financial policy was designed outside of public view. Greenspan outlined his new psychology to Clinton *alone* in the Governor's Mansion in Little Rock shortly after Clinton's election to his first term. No single economic policy could do more good for society than a drop in *long-term* interest rates. These rates matter most to businesses with large debts and to people paying mortgages. The Fed could control short-term interest rates but long-term rates would not drop unless the White House convinced "the bond market" that it was going to control the federal deficit.

Greenspan pictured bondholders and traders as "highly sophisticated," by which, he meant that they expected the federal budget deficit "to explode." With such vast federal expenditures, inflation would inevitably soar. In Greenspan's single-minded view—inherited from Arthur Burns—the budget deficits from government spending, not soaring oil prices, had induced the double-digit inflation of the late 1970s. Wary investors demanded a higher long-term return because of the expectations on deficits. This unfavorable spin on federal deficits was the new twist in the post-Reagan financial markets strategy of Wall Street.

With deficits under control, Greenspan said, market expectations would change. Bond traders would have more faith in their mantra, price stability, and long-term rates would drop. Since homeowners had increasingly used refinancing as a source of consumer credit, they would buy more automobiles, appliances, home furnishings, and other consumer goods. This borrowing and spending would wonderfully expand the economy. Moreover, as the bondholders got lower yields on bonds, they would shift money into the stock market, and stock prices would take off like a flock of geese. Finally, in this congenial environment, economic growth from deficit reduction would increase employment.

An Offer the White House Can't Refuse

By the end of more than two hours of "bonding," the new president-elect had signed onto Greenspan's version of Wall Street's financial strategy. Greenspanspeak might not have carried this day except for the deficit hawks circling Clinton's original agenda. The lead hawk and surely the one with a wingspan then rivaling Greenspan's, was Lloyd Bentsen, the Treasury Secretary designate. Leon E. Panetta, then the new budget director, also sounded the alarm that the budget deficit was shooting out of control. By the turn of the century, it would be $500 billion, "a truly unmanageable level."

The success of this Wall Street-Greenspan strategy would turn on the stimulus the economy would get from the promised fall in long-term interest rates. Alan Blinder, then a designated deputy director of the Council of Economic Advisers (CEA) and by 1995 Vice Chairman of the Fed, was among those at a critical agenda-setting meeting just 123 days before the inauguration. Blinder concluded that falling long-term interest rates could offset the adverse effect of a one point five percentage point lower economic growth rate from a reduction in government spending (and in the deficit) of $60 billion if the bond traders' inflation premium (based on expectations) evaporated. "But after ten years of fiscal shenanigans," warned Blinder, "the bond market will not likely respond."

At Blinder's revelation, Clinton's face turned red with anger and disbelief. "You mean to tell me that the success of the program and my re-election hinges on the Federal Reserve and a bunch of fucking bond traders?" The others at the meeting now agreed that indeed was the case (with expletives deleted)! At that defining moment Clinton perceived just how much of his fate was passing into the hands of the unelected, independent Alan Greenspan and "the bond market."

Then vice president-elect Albert Gore said that such "boldness" was the essence of Franklin D. Roosevelt's program. "Look at the 1930s," he reminded everyone. "Roosevelt was trying to help people," Clinton shot back. "Here we help the bond market, and we hurt the people who voted us in." Panetta told Clinton he had no choice. If he did not act, a balanced-budget amendment might pass Congress, forcing Clinton to surrender his presidency to a few members of Congress. Apparently, if the White House were to raise a white flag, hoisting it over the Reserve was far better than over the dome of Congress. Besides, Panetta warned, the reserve would likely raise short-term interest rates if the deficit kept going up. He neglected to refer to the latter as essentially Greenspanmail.

Clinton's economic team came to conclude that without Greenspan's cooperation they were doomed. This, of course, was Greenspan's intention. Bentsen went to Greenspan to assure him that the team had moved toward deficit reduction. "The Fed chairman, first among deficit hawks, smiled at the news." Bentsen concluded that Greenspan would be supportive within broad limits. Even the amount of the deficit reduction was set (at $140 billion) by Greenspan and passed along to Bentsen who passed it along to Clinton without attribution.

In only the second week of Clinton's presidency, Greenspan dropped his final bomb: After 1996, the interest on the debt would explode, and "a financial catastrophe" would follow. Bentsen was there along with Robert Rubin, then head of the National Economic Council and subsequently replacing Bentsen as Secretary of the Treasury. They agreed. With visions of stock market crashes, depression, and collapsing banks dancing in his head, Clinton assured the three that a major deficit reduction plan was already in the works. Clinton, the extraordinary mix of true Democrat, populist, Southern pulse-taker, man-of-the-people, and brainy policy student was out: Alan Greenspan and other deficit hawks and had swooped down and stolen Clinton's presidency.

The outcome for Clinton's own agenda was worse than he had thought at the time. Without Clinton's knowledge the Congress had decimated his investments because of the caps placed on spending for the years 1994 and 1995 as part of a 1990 budget deal. Once told of the effects of these caps, Clinton's temper erupts a second time. "I don't have a goddamn Democratic budget until 1996. None of the investment, none of the things I campaigned on." That, of course, was the case. In a separate account by former Secretary of Labor Robert Reich, Clinton stalks the room, fuming: "We're doing everything Wall Street wants!" That, too, was the case.

What were the immediate consequences of the Wall Street-Greenspan financial strategy? Gradually the 30-year bond rate *did* come down, from six point eight percent to below six percent, and the capital gains of bondholders went up. There followed a modest but steady expansion of GDP. Interest-sensitive spending on residential construction, plant and equipment investment, and consumer durables accounted for all of the growth that occurred in 1993. In those interest-rate sensitive sectors real GDP rose by eleven percent, while the non-interest-sensitive sectors showed virtually *no growth*. Greenspan and Bentsen credited the growth to "the financial markets strategy." Greenspan had claimed that each percentage point decline in the long-term rate would boost GDP by $50 to $75 billion: Bentsen rounded this up to $100 billion as a stronger selling point.

Fed Independence Remains a One-Way Street

But, now we know of the personal hypocrisy. The Fed's "independence" is based as much on convenience as necessity, ceded as it was during World War II and reclaimed during those Eisenhower years. Yet, renowned journalist Bob Woodward has Greenspan, sensitive to appearances contrary to "independence," agonizing over the propriety of his setting next to First Lady Hillary Clinton at the President's first State of the Union address. Nevertheless, Greenspan was there and looking more the peacock than the hawk, as well he should. Indirectly, Greenspan had done what the bond market had been given credit for: The Fed chairman had cuckolded Hillary's husband.

Unlike the Independence Avenue that runs from the Congress to the White House, the "Independence" of the Fed is a one-way street. In Woodward *and* Reich's reporting, Greenspan manipulates Clinton and Bentsen, and Bentsen manipulates everyone else. Greenspan's Fed, demanding that the White House and Congress never meddle in monetary policy, held the White House economic agenda in bondage. Greenspan, once simply a member of the Collective, is a charter member of the financial wealth holding class. One might suppose that the highly personal independence of Alan Greenspan would change, if not with events, with presidents. Not so. Rather, as we will soon enough learn, still another American president came to support Greenspan and Wall Street's strategy, which greatly favors the financial wealth holders.

7

GREENSPANMAIL REDEFINES THE NEW DEMOCRATS

Alan Greenspan does not deserve all the credit for the Wall Street-White House alliance. Robert Rubin remained a powerful force. Working quietly behind the scenes, he not only helped to persuade the president that federal deficit reduction was his top priority, but he also put a subtle pro-business stamp on Clinton's presidency. Greenspan wielded the greatest direct market power and authority because he not only set short-term interest rates, but greatly influenced the price of bonds at the U.S. Treasury. Still, he and Rubin were on the same page; it was a triple play.

Robert Rubin: From Wall Street to Bill to Alan

Robert Rubin had spent most of his working life at Goldman Sachs. Rubin has long been not only a New Democrat but also a centimillionaire exuding the calm, deliberate airs of the polished investment banker he once was and is again, at Citigroup. Beginning as an options trader in 1970, Rubin was, by the decade's end, one of a quartet of elite arbitrageurs known as the "four horsemen," one of whom was the notorious Ivan Boesky. Rubin went on to revive Goldman Sachs' bond department and become co-chairmen of the firm in 1990. As head of the National Economic Council, Rubin's responsibility was to coordinate the administration's economic policies.

During negotiations of Clinton's 1994 budget, Rubin had advised the president to ease up on his "tax the rich" rhetoric, which Rubin warned would increase "class divisiveness." His evident fear that the rich would rise up and revolt against the poor came too late; it had already happened! Secretary of Labor Reich suggested on

November 21, 1994 not only an attack on congressional Republicans for seeking a capital-gains tax cut and corporate tax cuts, but also that the presidential bully pulpit be used to tell people about the great increase in U.S. income and wealth concentration. Rubin blanches at such heresy.

"Mr. President," Rubin interrupts, "You've got to be *aw-ful-ly* careful to maintain the confidence of the financial markets. You don't want to sound as it you're blaming corporations." Later, on December 7, when Reich suggests eliminating some of the tax loopholes of large corporations, Rubin responds, "the financial markets would take it badly." Then, when Reich suggests that corporations should be required to count advertising outlays as an investment for tax purposes, saving the Treasury billions, Rubin responds, "the financial markets would take it very badly." When on Wall Street, Rubin buys and sells for the financial wealth holding class; when in public office, he has been one of its most influential spokesmen.

Greenspan Breaks His Promise

The Greenspan-White House alliance had the life span of a butterfly. President Clinton had trusted Alan Greenspan to keep his promise because the president had kept his: The first Clinton administration did more than reduce federal deficits, it generated federal budget surpluses. Yet, in January 1994 Greenspan went to the White House with a big surprise for Clinton and his economic advisers; inflation expectations were mounting, driving long-term rates to six point three percent. Clinton knew what was coming from Greenspan's Fed—higher interest rates—and he did not like it one bit.

By now, however, Robert Rubin had defined the New Democrat that Clinton wanted to be: pro-business but concerned for the poor and the middle class. If the administration was perceived as anti-business and anti-Wall Street, Rubin told the president, the administration would fall. Rubin helped to convince the president that he should not publicly criticize the Fed because of *its* independence; that would be *counterproductive* because then Greenspan would do the opposite. Bill had to play ball. Besides, deficit reduction would convince the bond market that inflationary expectations would never materialize and thus long-term interest rates would go lower; Clinton would be the big political winner. Instead, despite hitting a home run with the budget surpluses, the President struck out.

Two weeks later Greenspan twisted all the necessary arms on the FOMC to get a unanimous vote to raise short-term rates, with the Fed raising rates a third time on April 18, 1994. Three strikes: Clinton was out. The long-term benchmark rate moved to seven point four percent, higher than any time in Clinton's first term. Greenspan had broken his promise to the president to bring interest rates down if Clinton narrowed the deficit. Al Franken, the liberal and literal comic, might call the maestro "a liar"; Rubin called him a team player.

The Federal Reserve Board's official account, transmitted to Congress on February 21, 1995 is: "The Federal Reserve continued to tighten policy over the year and into 1995, as economic growth remained unexpectedly strong ...Developments in financial markets— for example, easier credit availability through banks and a decline in the foreign-exchange value of the dollar—may have muted the effects of the tightening of monetary policy." Firms and households were going deeper into debt (as Greenspan *had* promised) and the dollar was falling; however, these were now "reasons" for turning the monetary screws even tighter.

There was no public mention of a financial bubble. Yet at the May 17, 1994 FOMC meeting, the later released transcript has Greenspan once more addressing what he called "the financial bubble," noting that "the chances of our breaking the back of the economy at this point have to be pretty low." He went on and on about bubbles: "I think there's still a lot of bubble around; we have not completely eliminated it." (The release of these transcripts or *unedited* minutes of FOMC meetings was delayed five years.) At that meeting the maestro recommended a half point increase in the fed funds rate and got it with a unanimous vote. While Greenspan imagined a "soft landing" for the economy (or was it the stock market?) in his future, an angry President Clinton told his economic advisers to find a Democrat to put on the Federal Reserve Board.

Discussions within and outside the administration led to the nomination of Alan Blinder as vice chairman of the Board of Governors. Blinder, then at the Council of Economic Advisers (CEA), was a Keynesian whose earlier discourse on bond yields had provoked Clinton's expletive. His shift of Alan Blinder from the CEA to be the Fed's vice chair was not only an attempt to moderate Greenspan's policies, but to provide an heir apparent who would change the rules of the game. However, the Republican Congressional victory in 1994 ended White House hopes that Blinder could gain Senate approval and replace Greenspan. A carefully orchestrated effort by Greenspan and others to discredit Blinder on Wall Street as one too willing to tolerate "some inflation" to keep the economy growing now had the support of Congress. As to Wall Street, "the constituency for easy money—low rates—at the Fed has just lost one of its most outspoken champions," sniffed Fed Watcher Stephen S. Roach, chief economist at Morgan Stanley & Company, upon Blinder's departure from the Fed. Clinton had fought back, but to no avail.

The President's angry outbursts revealed his undeniable frustration. After all, his advisers tell him that a small and rich minority of the population in the bond market (the top ten percent held eighty-six percent of net financial assets and the top one percent, nearly half) would dictate the president's own agenda. The millionaires and billionaires—those *most active* in market speculation—had only 400,000 to 500,000 votes among themselves (not counting "dollar votes" of the investment bankers and other professionals on Wall Street). Despite this, most of Clinton's economic advisers embraced Wall Street and Greenspan's "financial markets strategy" as a new American icon, right up there with the Nike swoosh.

Greenspan, Keynes and the Role of Savings

Once we understand John Maynard Keynes, we can better understand the enormity of Greenspan's dominance over Clinton. We recall that Greenspan, an early-bird Keynesian, evolved into a radical free-market hawk under the influence of Ayn Rand and an anti-Keynesian under the more respectable influence of Arthur Burns. Along with the ideological baggage came occasional nods to Adam Smith and J.B. Say. After Greenspan's early flirtation, a Randian on Wall Street would have little motivation to return to Keynes, who saw a capitalistic world littered with market failures. The blooper of all market failures was the Great Depression that nearly benched capitalism, globally. In any case Greenspan and other central bankers fancy themselves as pragmatists beyond mere theories. As a game-playing master of the economic universe and an extremely conservative ideologue, maestro Greenspan could dispense with Keynes. That's too bad; pragmatism is not always useful.

There is much more to the theories of John Maynard Keynes than simply using government budget deficits to fight Great or Not-So-Great Depressions. Keynes took on J.B. Say and Say's law head-on. He sensed a fallacy; while a frugal household is good for the family, all families withholding their spending could be bad for the national economy. Potentially more embarrassing for Wall Street, the rich have a greater propensity to save because they have higher incomes and wealth. The poor and the middle class spend most if not all their incomes because they can afford only necessities.

Keynes agreed with Adam Smith that the purpose of production was consumption. Keynes did not even dispute Smith's idea that businesses depend upon other people's savings as sources of funds for real investment. Keynes nonetheless broke the direct link between savings and business investment envisioned by Smith and Say. Since, as Keynes put it, the households with net savings are different from the entrepreneurs building factories, what households plan to save has no directly necessary connection to what entrepreneurs plan to invest.

There is, if anything, a paradox in household thrift. When households intend to save less across an economy, they end up consuming more, and capitalists then have reason to spend more on inventories and for new buildings and outfitting of industrial plant. We see this effect in American data: during the past several decades about three-fourths of all corporate spending on capital goods and new factories came from the internal funds of the business—that is, from sales revenue dependent on consumers spending their incomes. The completely capitalistic act of buying capital goods adds to employment and incomes. Indeed, spending on capital goods has a multiplier effect; an extra dollar of business spending can generate two or more dollars of output and income, also multiplying employment. Then, higher than expected personal savings come from the rising employment and income created by the expansion of private industry. By intending to save less, households end up with more savings.

This conflict between what is good for a household and what is good for a nation has another potentially embarrassing lesson not only for Wall Street but for anyone who works bankers' hours. Smith and Say had household savings causing business investment. Keynes again turns the tables on the classical economists. In Keynes, real investment (inventories, tools, plant, and equipment) causes household savings and national private real saving. When businesses build more factories and buy more capital goods, construction and tool and die workers are hired and paid incomes that provide potentially more savings. A *nation* has not saved, however, until it has something to show for it—those factories and other capital that defines capitalism. After the dust from all this building activity settles, real investment has become *real saving*. Saving (the singular) has a different meaning from savings (the plural). In Keynes' theory and contrary to the Wall Street-Greenspan financial markets perspective, in the savings-investment lacunae the economic justification for extreme income and wealth disparities disappears.

Even when households spend a lot, we can't always count on corporations to invest a lot. Because of the uncertainty of profitable returns to entrepreneurial activity, Keynes believed that modern corporations would not always invest enough to assure full employment for labor. During times of extraordinarily low confidence, uncertainty regarding entrepreneurial returns and bond prices (and hence long-term interest rates) is lethal, leading to a collapse in business investment and final total demand. Keynes called final total demand, *effective* demand, the demand materializing, not only in the sales of capital goods, but in the sales of clothing, autos, houses, and battleships. Keynes, writing his *General Theory of Employment, Interest, and Money* during the Great Depression of the 1930s, attributed those frightening conditions to a collapse in business investment and inadequate effective demand.

Moreover, wrote Keynes, a rudderless economic ship of state may sink without sensible government budgetary policies. When Keynes was writing his General Theory during the Great Depression, of course, free enterprise capitalism appeared not simply sinking, but going to the bottom of the turbulent economic seas.

The Conversion of the New Democrats

The conversion of the Clinton administration from Keynesianism to Greenspanism is complete in the 1995 *Economic Report of the President*, written by Clinton's Council of Economic Advisers (CEA). The CEA dramatically details the true reason for federal deficit reductions through cut-backs in Clinton's domestic agenda, just as if the President has not done enough for Alan Greenspan and the financial wealth holders: "A primary economic reason for reducing the federal deficit is to increase national saving, in the expectation that increased saving will, in turn, increase national investment in physical capital...." National saving causes investment; Clinton's economists have turned Keynes on his head. In this way, the *Report* also embraces Say's law in which the savings of the financial wealth holders comprise not only a social virtue but the direct and reliable route to greater real capital accumulation. Wall Street and Greenspan could have written the message—in truth, they did!

By early 1995 signs of an economic slowdown also appeared. The same parts of the economy very sensitive to interest rate reductions are equally or even more sensitive to interest rate increases. Moreover, a Republican-dominated Congress was pushing for deficit reduction though spending cuts and greatly reduced tax rates for the rich, precisely the arithmetic favored by Wall Street and Greenspan's ideology. Meanwhile, President Clinton was taking a beating in the polls, despite the only significant deficit reductions since the Nixon Administration. And, there was an ongoing re-election campaign in which Clinton appeared to be the underdog, partly attributable to the effects of the Greenspan-Clinton one-way alliance. Despite the President's side of the financial markets strategy being in disarray, job improvements during the campaign, Clinton's wholesale adoption of the Republican agenda, and a lackluster campaign from pre-Viagra Bob Dole was sufficient to re-elect Clinton in 1996.

Though Blinder's resignation as vice chairman of the Fed left two unfilled seats among the seven governors, the GOP's capture of Congress and Greenspan's behind-the-back arm-twisting on Wall Street guaranteed that President Clinton would nominate Greenspan for another term beginning March 1996. Clinton's first choice to replace Blinder as vice chair was Felix Rohatyn, managing director of Lazard Frères investment house *and* a liberal Democrat. Rohatyn not only has written extensively about his concern for financial fragility but also had called for the Fed to worry less about goods inflation. He, too, could not win Senate confirmation over Wall Street's hostility. Instead, Greenspan probably helped select Clinton's other two Fed nominees—the OMB director Alice Rivlin, her hawkish wingtips now touching those of Greenspan, tapped for vice chair, and St. Louis economic consultant Laurence H. Meyer, as a governor. Both agreed that the economy can't grow any faster than about two point five percent yearly without rekindling the fires of inflation. Later, to the credit of each, they moderated that stance.

The Fate of Clinton's Second-Term Economic Policy is Sealed

The nearly complete capitulation of the U.S. to Wall Street and Greenspan comes after Clinton's "victory," his re-election. The 1997 *Economic Report of the President* claims that interest rates would have been higher had deficit reductions not taken place, ignoring the unmistakable fact that Greenspan had *raised* the fed funds rate nearly fifty percent against inflation's ghost in 1994—*after* the deficit reduction legislation. Though Clinton had *reduced* budget deficits steadily, interest rates *went up*, .not only in 1994, but also in 1995 and 1997. *Greenspan* had *raised* interest rates in the face of *declining* federal deficits. Despite sacrificing employment for imaginary inflation, the Clinton Administration continued to pursue the Wall Street-Greenspan agenda. Three years of compelling evidence mounted against the necessity of the trade-off; every estimate of the conservatives-inspired natural rate of unemployment had predicted a rising inflation rate, but it did not rise.

Going forward in time but not in solid thinking, even the 1998 *Economic Report* fails to dismiss the highly unreliable natural rate of unemployment idea, despite a quickening in its name to NAIRU (non-accelerating-inflation rate of unemployment). Moreover, this report, like all Clinton-era reports, carefully avoids a serious discussion of monetary policy, much less any criticism of Alan Greenspan's policies. President Clinton's reverence for Fed independence contrasts sharply with Greenspan's total disregard for the independence of the White House!

Greenspan's Edge over the Democrats

When all is said, using traditional Democratic Party language to rationalize Greenspan's financial markets strategy is devilishly difficult. How did the New Democrats come to this sorry state of economic affairs?

Clinton's choices were limited by Greenspanmail. If Clinton had not gotten the deficits down, Greenspan *would* have *immediately* boosted up short-term rates, rather than waiting for a time. And, as we know, the chairman could not be replaced for "political reasons," but presidents can be. Fed independence coupled with the unchallenged power of Wall Street and Alan Greenspan carried the day. The cost to President Clinton and the Democrats was the destruction of their entire domestic economic agenda. There also would be continuing costs to ordinary Americans—part of the Greenspan legacy.

Ironically, the dependence of the Fed on Wall Street's private investment bankers would consolidate Greenspan's power in Washington, D.C. That extension of his powers also would set the fate of the second Clinton administration, much as Greenspan and his U.S. Treasury colleagues had decided the fate of the first administration. We next turn to those forces.

8

FED AND WHITE HOUSE
DEPENDENCE
ON WALL STREET INVESTMENT
BANKERS

Federal Reserve independence is less than pure in many ways. The takeover of the economic and financial agenda of the White House by Alan Greenspan and the Reserve was audacious, but there is much more to the hypocrisy—the duplicity of the one-way street. An element of impurity is the long-time relationship of the Fed and the U.S. Treasury to Wall Street and the global financial community; it is a connection that decided the fate not just of interest-rate policy but of broader issues during Bill Clinton's presidency. More important, the ideology of Wall Street and Greenspan was embraced as a natural and comfortable base in a White House and a Congress dominated by neoconservatives after the "election" of George W. Bush.

Consider an example of the revolving door between Washington, D.C. and Wall Street bankers. Robert Rubin, Clinton's second Treasury Secretary, was an investment banker before and after his appointment. Rubin returned to Wall Street to chair Citigroup's executive committee. Citigroup, as it has turned out, is now the world's largest bank, one of the all-purpose mega-banks created by Bill Clinton's 1998 deregulation legislation authored by Rubin with advanced regulatory approval from Fed Chairman Alan Greenspan. While Citigroup is paying huge fines (dwarfed by its market value) for its misconduct in the Enron and other scandals, it is sufficiently dominant globally that its stock is generally rated a "buy."

As noted, Greenspan and company's devotion to free private financial markets is total, *except* for *their* Roark-like interventions. Only when a private financial institution encounters a crisis, which has often been of the chairman's creation, does the Fed intervene. And, as American finance has gone global, so has the reach of the Federal Reserve System and Citigroup. Worse, as American finance has become more innovative, it has become riskier. Ironically, Alan Greenspan's effective lobbying for deregulation of financial markets has altered the connections among the Fed and what used to be exclusively "bankers."

OLIPHANT © (1999) UNIVERSAL PRESS SYNDICATE. Reprinted with permission. All rights reserved.

What Wall Street Investment Bankers Do

The Fed's cozy relationship with Wall Street investment bankers both preceded and followed the Clinton administration. Traditionally, the most powerful firms on Wall Street have been the major investment-banking houses, the largest and most prestigious being Salomon, Morgan Stanley, Merrill Lynch Securities Inc., First Boston, J.P. Morgan Securities Inc., Bear, Stearns & Co., and Goldman Sachs. Salomon is now part of Citigroup Global Markets Inc., following a merger with Smith Barney, while First Boston has merged with Credit Suisse. When knowledgeable financiers speak of those banking houses, they still talk respectfully in hushed tones; they have that great Wall Street tool, "contacts with potential buyers."

The country's largest corporations, state and local governments, and even the U.S. Treasury, come to these firms for money in return for their new issues of bonds and stocks. Although it is not widely understood, businesses and governments only raise cash when they issue newly minted stocks and bonds. When these securities are re-sold in the retail market, only the ownership of the securities changes hands: The corporation or government receives no additional funds, only the assurance that any new issues will have a ready (or not) market. This distinction between the primary financial markets (new issues) and the secondary financial markets (re-sales) is like the difference between the new and used car markets. When General Motors used cars are resold, it receives no revenue except for those it re-finances. In this there is a paradox to which we will return: More often than not, the greater the rewards from financial activities, the less the real investment in things like new factories and new machines.

Investment Bankers' Ties to Monetary Policy

We return to bonds, since the U.S. and other treasuries do not issue equities. Investment bankers, going all the way back to Pierpont Morgan do not place new bond issues as a charitable act. They fully expect to make a profit. Since most borrowers reach agreements in which the investment banker guarantees a successful sale (to those contacts), by that they *underwrite* the issue. At the same time, the underwriter assumes the issuer's risk of being unable to sell the entire issue. If, God forbid, something goes wrong in the financial markets, the underwriter must absorb any resulting losses. Investment bankers do not like this to happen because the underwriter's profit from the bond issue comes from the difference between the price the investment banker pays for the bonds and the price at which they sell the bonds to investors. This difference—highly regarded by the underwriter—is the spread or differential. The bankers have considerable control over this spread because buyers usually cannot afford to open more than one account and thereby cross-check offering prices.

Still, any untoward event disrupting a bond sale is a nightmare for the underwriter. Even after the initial sale, normally the underwriter holds a goodly value of the bonds on its own account. Suddenly, a currency crisis might break out, as it did during August 1998 in Russia, causing interest rates to shoot up ("spike" is the word often used). Since the interest payments or coupon rate had already been set, the Russian bonds' selling price plunged, raising the measured yield. (Lowering the selling price of the bonds not only increases the cost of the borrowing, it reduces the funds received, be it by the government or by Russian firms.) Worse from the underwriters' perspective, the spread and the underwriters' profit on new issues narrowed. Worse still, they knew that any new issue would not be fully subscribed or sold. As a result of the Russian Crisis, Salomon quickly experienced $60 million in Russia-related bond losses. It is little wonder that Salomon once tried to corner the U.S. Treasuries market.

Being highly specialized and prized, investment bankers are among the few. From an already small population of dominant investment and commercial bankers, the Federal Reserve Bank of New York selects a still smaller group of securities dealers and commercial banks as *primary* dealers and brokers in its securities. In August 2004, the New York Fed had designated only 22 primary dealers. These private dealers are, in turn, brokers for large private customers, such as commercial banks, insurance companies, large finance companies, and wealthy clients. As exclusive dealers, these broker-dealers trade in U.S. Government securities with the Federal Reserve Bank of New York that, in turn, trades on behalf of the Federal Open Market Committee (FOMC) of the Federal Reserve System. These special investment banks, the primary dealers, work the other side of the market for the FOMC.

These bankers have achieved great importance because they are the linchpin to the conduct of monetary policy—that is, the setting of the fed funds rate. The FOMC transmits its fed funds rate objective to the N.Y. Fed. Suppose the goal is to raise the fed funds rate, which is the overnight lending rate for private bank reserves held at the

Fed banks. The New York Fed then will sell Government securities in the secondary or resale market through the primary dealers. This sale decreases reserves of the private commercial banking system so that banks have fewer funds to lend overnight. To ration the reserves (fed funds), the fed funds rate is raised. A net purchase of securities from the banks adds to private bank reserves and lowers the fed funds rate. As noted, other interest rates in the banking system and elsewhere are tied to movements in the fed funds rate.

The primary dealer designation gives special status to these firms; these private investment banks are effectively subsidiaries of the Federal Reserve System. The 2004 list of such primary dealers includes the usual Who's Who of suspects—Bear, Stearns, Citigroup Global Markets, Credit Suisse First Boston, Goldman Sachs, J.P. Morgan Securities, Merrill Lynch Government Securities, and Morgan Stanley. The New York Fed once had a Bank's dealer surveillance unit, but when the investment banks complained that this implied regulation by the New York Fed, the focus of the surveillance was shifted to The Market, which is quietly impersonal and, of course, God. These investment banks with church-like office suites adorned in fine old antiques, precious artwork and silver tea services until recently had no public presence in the retail brokerage business.

During the Great Bull Market, the names of the old investment banking firms combined with the once lowly retail firms began to read like law partnerships. For example, Morgan Stanley joined forces with Dean Witter Discover, a blue-stocking-meets-blue-collar merger. The new company had Dean Witter selling mutual funds at Sears' stores, a "socks and stocks" play at a retailer having difficulty selling socks. The old-line firms remained devoted to bonds in one way or another, and retreated from the banking "supermarket" model by 2005. Morgan Stanley's retail operation then was valued at about $6 billion, while its unit that includes traditional investment banking was valued at $40 billion. Morgan Stanley now appears to be refocusing on investment banking, where historically it has enjoyed a twenty to twenty-five percent rate of return.

The Investment Bankers Move into Clinton's White House and Implement Greenspan's Proposed White House Budgets

Since federal deficits are funded by the issuance of U.S. Treasury bonds, investment bankers are going to be involved with White House budgetary policies—taxes and spending. Although he was merely President of the United States, Bill Clinton agonized over his balanced budget agreements with Congress during early 1997. He was confronted with Greenspanmail across a broad spectrum of his policies because of the close ties of the U.S. Treasury, the Federal Reserve and private investment bankers. Not only were investment bankers natural allies of Alan Greenspan, they fully populated the Clinton administration.

In December 1996, as the president made his cabinet appointments for his second term, he not only named Robert Rubin to replace Bentsen as Secretary of Treasury, but as "captain of the team." Rubin and the other men responsible for getting the president's budget through Congress had left successful careers in investment banking. Erskine Bowles, a venture capitalist from North Carolina, became chief of the White House staff. The new head of the OMB, Franklin Raines, helped run mortgage giant Fannie Mae. All these bankers could slip unnoticed into a conservative Republican administration; some Democrats were wishing that they had. In any case, they signed onto the Greenspan-inspired 1997 Budget Reconciliation Act and capital gains tax reductions that greatly and disproportionately benefited wealthy families.

Once a *lender* to governments as head of Goldman Sachs, as President Clinton's Secretary of Treasury Rubin went hat in hand to his old firm as a borrower. As U.S. Secretary of Treasury, Rubin continued to fret greatly over what the financial markets might "think." He, like Greenspan, considered markets sufficiently smart to be their own guardians, except when they were in trouble. Clinton would send the Treasury Secretary and Greenspan, who remained close friends, to San Francisco in early September 1998 to negotiate with Japan's finance minister, ironically, attempting to push Japan toward an expansionary fiscal policy, while Clinton was pursuing a frugal fiscal policy.

In the end the centerpiece of the 1997 tax bill signed by Clinton was a cut in capital gains taxes and other tax benefits for the rich. The richest one percent of households once again benefited by far the most, with each paying $16,000 less in taxes. The bottom twenty percent of U.S. households saw their taxes *rise* by an average of $40 a year. The second twenty percent saw no change, and the middle twenty percent gained only $150 a year. New Democrats, it has been said, are the pragmatists who are able to compromise with the GOP. By that standard, if by no other, Bill Clinton became the most compromised Democrat president in history.

Greenspan Eclipses Clinton's Legacy

Just as Alan Greenspan has recently anguished over his legacy in his final official term, President Bill Clinton sought ways to some kind of legacy. Out-bought by the investment bankers outside his administration and outnumbered by Greenspan and investment bankers on the *inside*, in his second term Clinton abandoned domestic economic policy concerns and was looking to foreign policy achievements as a way to elevate his place in history. He had fought Greenspan and Wall Street and had lost, first, as President-Elect, turning domestic economic policy over to Greenspan, then, turning the White House over to a Greenspan's investment-banking allies. Besides, by September 1998, a hypocritically devout Republican-dominated House of Representatives was moving toward impeachment of the President. Clinton had been much closer to having his way with Monica Lewinsky than with Alan Greenspan.

In any non-sexual contest with Bill Clinton, Greenspan proved to be the better man. While Clinton floundered, Chairman Greenspan surfaced not only as the most powerful economic and financial policy leader in the world, but also as the acknowledged global spokesman for deregulation and privatization. Within the Reserve, he had minimized challenges to his decisions by deft maneuvering. His anti-inflation phobia has won raves from the wealthy and from Wall Street generally, even when deflation came onto the global scene. The down-payment on income inequality was crafted out of a financial markets strategy that included tax cuts for the rich orchestrated by the maestro and the investment bankers. By his third term, Greenspan was answering to no one. He had even more power over the American economy and much of the global economy.

The Dependence Continues to This Day

The Federal Reserve and the U.S. Treasury's close friendship with the bond dealers and brokers on Wall Street continues to this day even though underwriting, the profits center, was temporarily outrun by the bulls in the rapidly expanding resale market of the 1990s. The subsequent collapse of stock markets at the end of the 1990s, corporate scandals, and shaky financial recoveries by 2004 shifted Wall Street's focus back toward investment banking. At the work-a-day level, like Robert Rubin and Lawrence Summers before them, Treasury secretaries Paul O'Neill and John Snow under George W. Bush had to cooperate with Wall Street investment banks in the placement of U.S. federal debt. Alan Greenspan had to continue to rely on a few select investment banks and dealers in the conduct of the Fed's main business, monetary policy.

We cannot avoid an important concern even if Alan Greenspan continues to evade it. U.S. Treasury and Federal Reserve dependence on Wall Street and a few investment bankers is a remarkable feature of a system in which the Federal Reserve maintains its one-way *political* independence. At Greenspan's urging and protection, off-Wall Street, off-balance sheet hedge funds have not only proliferated, but also are taking on new roles as lenders. Already, they are involved in various kinds of speculations in U.S and foreign Treasury securities. Will the U.S. Treasury and the Federal Reserve System become dependent on hedge funds to underwrite the U.S. federal debt and maintain financial stability? Since the Federal Reserve has given enormous power and prestige to Wall Street, what will happen when that power and prestige is transferred to largely unregulated hedge funds that have already endangered global financial stability? These questions provide sufficient reasons to consider the derivatives giving rise to hedge funds and, later, the anatomy of hedge funds themselves.

9

THE FABLE OF THE GOLDILOCKS ECONOMY

The process of easing monetary policy ... had to be closely controlled and generally gradual, because of the constraint imposed by the marketplace's acute sensitivity to inflation. ... At the end of the 1970s, investors became painfully aware that they had underestimated the economy's potential for inflation. As a result, monetary policy in recent years has had to remain alert to the possibility that an ill-timed easing could be undone by a flare-up of inflation expectations, ...

Alan Greenspan, testimony before the Committee on Banking, Finance, and Urban Affairs of the U.S. House of Representative, July 20, 1993.

Greenspan's statement and others like it serve as the preamble to the Goldilocks Economy. Shortly thereafter, Greenspan and the Fed began that long series of interest-rate increases as a pre-emptive strike against inflationary expectations, which, they believed, would lead to even higher interest rates and economic recession. Greenspan has always been willing to risk recession to avoid even imagined goods inflation. Although fairytales are supposedly written for children, this fable was designed for adult financial wealth holders. Since the nineteenth century could not be restored, Goldilocks became the new Gold Standard for Alan Greenspan. Out of Goldilocks came the Greenspan Standard indicators for stellar economic performance—hyper-inflation in asset prices and zero inflation in goods prices.

Goods inflation, the traditional measure of inflation often thought to be tied to rising wages, strikes fear deep in the heart of the financial wealth holding class. The perceived enemy of financial asset appreciation is inflation in the prices of commodities of plain, ordinary manufactured goods and capital goods. As long as the real economy of autos, clothing and movie tickets is kept soft, the unemployment rate adequately elevated, goods inflation will be mild and financial asset inflation substantial. The wealth holders have absolutely no fear of inflation in bond and stock prices, From this definition of the good economy came, by sometime in 1995, the idea of the *Goldilocks Economy*, an economy based not on myth, but on a mildly twisted though beloved, fairytale.

Once upon a time there were three bears: Papa Bear, Mama Bear, and Baby Bear. Papa Bear had a large bond portfolio, Mama Bear held a great amount of stocks, and Baby Bear was studying to become a central banker like Alan Greenspan. Baby Bear was reading a comic book on the conduct of monetary policy published by the New York Federal Reserve Bank.

"I think the economy is too hot," said Papa Bear. "Auto sales went up at an annual rate of eight percent last month, whereas the expected increase was only two percent; the data was published in the *Wall Street Journal* this morning."

"Well, I think you are mistaken," said Mama Bear. "Auto sales may have gone up but, when I logged onto my computer, PC prices were way down. I believe the economy is too cold. I'm going to sell all my stocks!"

"Based on what I just learned from the New York Fed's comic book," up-spoke Baby Bear, "I think you're both wrong. When strong sales in one part of the economy are offset by weak prices in personal computers, the Fed chair calls those the result of 'productivity improvements'; when he senses a lack of direction of the economy up or down, he follows a neutral monetary policy, keeping real interest rates where they are. I think the economy is *just right*!"

Goldilocks, a bond broker, was simpatico with Baby Bear's temperature reading.

"I suggest you take Baby Bear's temperature as the correct reading for the economy," advised Goldilocks, as she teased her blond curls. "The economy *is* just right."

"Sell me more bonds," thundered Papa Bear.

"Sell me more stocks," whispered Mama Bear.

And the Good News Bears all lived richly ever after.

The Financial Good News

Two eras in the American twentieth century, the Jazz Age and the Great Bull Market of the 1980s–1990s, were not only defined by an extraordinary exuberance in the financial markets but by two unique, shared features. First, financial asset prices more often than not were judged the most important measures of economic well-being. Second, bond and stock prices moved upward in a tandem. But, the 1990s was not the end of the Goldilocks fable, after the collapse of the dot-com and tech stock bubble Alan Greenspan and the Federal Reserve attempted to write another fairytale ending for the wealth holding class. Although securities holders did well in this second telling, wealthy owners of speculative real estate were doing much better—to which we will return.

Although goods mostly are being manufactured in Asia and imported into the United States, the Great Bull Market was made in America and exported. Prices of U.S. government and corporate bonds began an unmistakable upward ascent along with the Dow in the 1980s. Even the abrupt interruptions in this overall upward trend were instructive; on those rare occasions when the twins did go their separate ways, repercussions were dramatic. Falling bond prices (rising bond yields) and rising stock prices preceded the aforementioned crash of 1987, the mini-crash of 1989, and a series of mini-crashes beginning during the summer of 1997. Otherwise, the trend is not only unmistakable but may be replayed before Greenspan retires.

What began as a pattern of thinking became an obsession of well-to-do citizens and public officials around the mid-1990s. To understand what Wall Street means by "good news," consider some of the highs and lows in the financial markets. Though the bond and stock markets remained highly volatile through 1995–1998, lurching down with each rumor of an improving real economy and up with well-received "bad news," the Dow gained twenty-six percent during 1995 and another thirty-three point five percent during 1996, the best two-year showing for the barometer in twenty years. The bull continued to roar in 1997; the Dow cracked the 7000 barrier by Valentine's Day, up nine percent for the year and rising at an annual rate of sixty-seven percent! Then, the Dow began what was to be a 700-point retreat beginning March 11, 1997. However, the Dow still had heart.

Coming back, after bond prices took off, the Dow billowed 500 points during seven business days in late April and early May. On April 29, the U.S. Labor Department reported that Americans' wages and benefits rose a timid zero point six percent in the first quarter: The bond market soared and the Dow bounded 179.01 points. On May 3, following an announcement by the Clinton administration and congressional Republican leaders to an agreement to balance the budget by 2002, Scott Bleier, chief investment strategist at Prime Charter Ltd., tells us, "It's been said for the last two years by Alan Greenspan himself that if there is a budget agreement reached it will be rewarded with potentially lower [interest] rates." And, of course, *lower* interest rates mean *higher* bond prices. The Dow leaped 94.72 points. Alan Greenspan had kept his promise to Wall Street. On May 16, however, market players were hit with the "bad news" that housing construction had jumped an unexpected two point six percent in April and that consumers' confidence was surprisingly strong. The Dow shed its nearly 140 points. .

Persistently "good news" came none too soon for these *Good News Bears*. "The market believes the economy is slowing, and in the meanwhile profits will be good and any increase in interest rates will be modest," glowed A. Marshall Acuff, market strategist at Smith Barney, Harris Upham & Co. "Wall Street isn't too concerned about the economy," he added. Bond prices rose and the Dow shot up, gaining 135.64 and settling at another record high at 7711.47. Another piece of "good news" was a third straight month of declines in retail sales. Continued weakness in retail sales (despite bullishness in Ralph Lauren Polo shirts) and negligible wage growth were sufficient "to bolster the case that the Fed will keep rates steady through their July meeting," said James Solloway, research director at Argus Research. In contrast, a six-year *runaway inflation in financial asset prices* was to be greatly admired.

Our Deeply Felt Concerns for Bond Holders and Investment Bankers

We can't move past the good news bears without conveying some compassion for a put upon tough tiny minority, the two to four percent of families holding bonds. Their fears and those of their investment-banker friends are not to be taken lightly. The bondholders' common anxiety is not about their own employment that is secure or the employment of others that is not. Their anxiety is manifestly about inflation in the prices of ordinary goods and services—of Fords, denims, a steak dinner, and a beer because goods inflation causes bond prices to fall. Sometimes, when their hands tremble as they hold the bond prices' page of the day's *Wall Street Journal*, they quaver for good reason. As for Alan Greenspan and other central bankers to come, they must worry about keeping the bond market open for Fed business.

Worse, the lives of the bond holders and the investment bankers have become dreadfully complex. It is not simply the goods inflation they fear. They fear *what the Federal Reserve will do in its attempt to slow goods inflation*. They fear that the Fed will take actions to raise interest rates (lowering bond prices) in its pious devotion to price stability; this fear remained palpable even as the ghost of goods inflation in 1995 vaporized, and still later, stock prices plunged. Even after an interim of uncharacteristic concern with deflation, Greenspan's tortured rhetoric of 2005 often signaled inflation just around the corner as the FOMC moved the fed funds rate target slowly but relentlessly away from one percent and toward four point five percent. Any *hint* of interest rate hikes by the wizard of Wall Street can cause a stampede of bears from the bond market to seek temporary shelter in the stock market and, far worse, a capital loss for the bond holder. This Goldilocks effect has been so predictable that when it lapsed between the summers of 2004 and 2005, Greenspan christened it a "conundrum." If we are wealthy and we own a lot of bonds, we have good reason to be worried.

Suppose instead we work for a living, not out of desire, but out of sheer need. Should we also be worried?

What About the Rest of the Animal Kingdom?

In the Goldilocks Economy, the job and income prospects necessarily are tepid for those working for a living. In the greatest economic perversion of capitalism since the 1920s, unearned incomes from financial assets generally moved in the opposite direction as the incomes of working people. The rich put their accumulated personal savings into play in financial markets where Alan Greenspan and the Federal Reserve guaranteed returns to be higher than in the production economy in which slow growth or "sloth" was the order of the day. Wonderfully, too, those whose incomes are exclusively or mostly from capital gains, bond interest payments, and stock dividends are immune to the calamity of employment.

Even Alan Greenspan and Goldilocks could not keep stock and bond prices rising without interruption. As we explore the great collapse of a financial bubble too big to last, we nonetheless still find this upside-down Alice-in-Wonderland capitalism continuing to widen an already great chasm between the haves and the have-nots. The American and much of the global economy have still to recover from the aftermath of the effects of a Goldilocks Economy still in play. While the makeup of asset returns shifted somewhat from securities to housing, we find that Goldilocks never really went away.

The embrace of the Goldilocks Economy as the path to the Greenspan Standard has split the economic world—not only in the U.S. but globally—between the real economy and a casino economy. What remains of capitalism revolves around the use of personal savings for speculative gains, while public policy favoring slow economic growth and minimal wages for workers has transformed the American Dream into a nightmare. The world of finance—first, excessive credit fueling financial asset inflation and, recently, excessive credit fueling housing asset inflation—has crowded out the normal production of ordinary goods and services and thus full employment.

As it turns out, an economy never too hot and never too cold made things uncomfortable for ordinary workers.

10

THE WOLF AT THE DOOR OF ORDINARY WORKERS

Q: What's your purpose in life?
A: To stamp out inflation.
Q: Even if that means high unemployment?
A: You bet.
Q: Even if it requires slow growth and stagnant wages?
A: Right you are.

Robert B. Reich, *Locked in the Cabinet* (New York: Alfred A. Knopf, 1997). These were the questions that Robert Reich, Bill Clinton's Secretary of Labor, wanted to ask Alan Greenspan when they met for lunch in 1993.

In a financial markets strategy aimed to please Wall Street and a few financial wealth holders, some people are bound to get hurt. Goods inflation was demonized as the enemy, only to become the excuse. Rising economic inequality was inevitable. Those who held financial assets would initially benefit greatly; almost a decade and a half later, those who work for a living are still waiting for adequate permanent jobs and a sustained living wage.

After his first luncheon meeting with the Chairman, then Secretary of Labor Robert Reich describes Greenspan as a little man—slightly stooped, balding, large nose, wide lips, a wry smile, and wearing thick glasses. He is the man we always see on CNN crossing the street from the Fed building on his way to testify before the Congress. Greenspan is Jewish and from New York and reminds Reich of his uncle Louis but with the voice of his uncle Sam. Reich, a Jewish liberal then and today, actually likes the guy. Yet, at the end of the lunch, the Secretary realizes that Greenspan had gotten exactly what he wanted and Reich never asked him the questions he intended to, and didn't get the answers Reich imagined he would give.

In another fable with a darker side, Reich's uncle Alan Greenspan is a wolf in grandmother's clothing. Little Red Riding Hood is a hapless Wal-Mart employee on her way to work but about to be had for lunch, much like Secretary of Labor Reich. "Grandmother" wants the Wal-Mart employee to be subservient, paid little, given few benefits, but highly productive. Increasingly American workers have had no choice except to mix their metaphors—to sleep with labor's enemy to keep the wolf away from grandmother's door.

"Good News" Turns Bearish for Ordinary Workers

"Good news" on Wall Street was not always bad news for working stiffs. During the quarter century immediately after World War II, members of congress, presidents, and even heads of the Federal Reserve were concerned that everyone wanting a job had full-time employment and a living wage. The shift in concerns away from the masses and toward the financial elite is so dramatic, we would expect someone to have noticed it. Yet, growing income and wealth inequalities are presently invisible in American politics. Judging from the media and the political attention they receive, the most important issues to the typical American include not only assuring the continued appreciation in financial market prices and high-end housing, but ending federal budget deficits when they are "caused" by income and health support for typical families.

Under the Greenspan Standard tax *cuts* for the wealth holders and tax *increases* for those on social security are equally desirable. The Reserve's favoritism to the financial community and its antipathy for the well-being of typical families is so obvious, we wonder why its monetary operations remain stealthy. The answer is equally clear but no less painful. To those who control the financial levers and thus the global economy, arrogance is a natural aspect of superior pecuniary intelligence. Those who hold no or few assets are simply not focused on financial markets; they don't speak the same language as those on CNBC "Power Lunch" or the Fed watchers. When I asked an auto repairman (being in the business) whether I should buy put options in

General Motors, he replied "Your best option is to *put* the money into new brakes on your car, though it only has 25,000 miles on it."

We have even less reason to doubt the passion of the financial community in pursuing its goals. While *financial asset inflation* seems an illogical goal for those who have no or few financial assets, it is an ideologically pure objective for wealth holders. By the mid-1990s, when Goldilocks first took full flight, Wall Street was telling us that the stock market had become "democratic" because most American families now owned stocks. Already, Alan Greenspan was talking of the virtues of privatization of Social Security. Wall Street is rather clear on this: buying and selling securities is *hard work* whether you have a $10 million or a $50 billion portfolio. Alan Greenspan did not get that harried and worried look from picking oranges and tomatoes alongside migrant labor.

It is Bad News That "Trickles Down," Not the Savings of the Rich

The terrible truth is that ordinary workers are unlikely to earn enough in wages to accumulate much in the way of financial wealth. The main asset of workers is their primary residence, but it serves a primary function as necessary shelter, not as a wealth generator. Their incomes, until an uncertain retirement in a world of diminishing private pensions and Social Security under assault, generally depend on work effort. Since at least the early 1980s real wages and benefits have gone soft for Americans, while the income from financial assets and, more recently, second and third homes, has soared.

Undeniably, the incomes of the rich have quickly floated much higher even as those of ordinary workers have slipped beneath the high tide of Wall Street and Greenspan. Those who work for a living in the U.S. have seen little or no progress during the past three decades. Moreover, earlier trends have been reversed. The real income of the median family (half had more, half had less) doubled between 1947 and 1973, but rose only twenty-two percent from 1973 to 2003, with much of that gain due to wives' entering the paid labor force or working longer hours, but not from earning higher wages. Those higher up in the income ranks did much better. Since 1973 the average income of the top one percent of Americans *has* doubled, while the income of the top zero point one percent has *tripled*. The higher you go, the greater the increase in inequality. Those 13,000 or so households in the top zero point zero one percent had an *average* income of $10.8 million in 2002, having increased nearly four times.

The CEOs of the corporations paying modest wages to their workers have been doing much better. In a survey of 367 CEOs by *Business Week*, April 18, 2005, median pay was $9.6 million (again, half got more, half got less). It has not always been so. The ratio of CEO pay to average workers pay has gone from 40-to-1 in the 1970s to 361-to-1 in 2003. These changing ratios imply that the quality of CEOs have increased nine times faster than the quality of their employees, raising serious questions regarding their hiring practices. Of course, much of the gain at the highest levels is from the ownership of securities, including stock options. Still, 40 of the CEOs in the 2005 *Business Week* survey took home over $20 million, even excluding the windfalls from the exercise of stock options.

According to those, such as Mr. Greenspan, who not only helped design Reagan's tax cuts for the very rich as well as the tax-challenged policies of George W. Bush, this inequality is best preserved. In 2000, the last year in which the government will release such data, the 400 taxpayers with the highest incomes (at a minimum of $87 million) paid income, Medicare and Social Security taxes amounting to about the same percentage of their incomes as people making $50,000 to $75,000. Worse, those earning more than $10 million yearly paid a *smaller* share of their income in taxes than those making $100,000 to $200,000.

According to Wall Street, J.B. Say and Alan Greenspan, the savings of those at the top of the income mountain trickle down to benefit those clinging to a precipice lower down. Bad news, not income, has trickled down. Some very rich became super-rich and many very poor became direly poor. The trend toward more equality of a half century beginning during the 1930s has reversed.

Otherwise, It's All About Wealth (Net Worth)

Wealth is always less equally distributed than income. The concentration of wealth was revealed in a 1995 survey at the Federal Reserve Board. Fully ninety-seven percent of all U.S. families directly held *no* bonds. Some sixty percent of households did not own *any* bonds *or* stocks, and of the forty percent that did (either directly or indirectly), most owned very little. For example, the median holdings for those in the bottom fifth of household income owned only $4300 (in *2001 dollars*) in stocks, mostly held (indirectly) in pension and mutual funds. (The *median* is such that half of those families had more than $4300 and half had less.) *Half* the value of all stock held by U.S. families was held by the best-off five percent. A tiny sliver, the best-off one percent of the wealth holders, held about *half* the value of *all* financial assets.

Worse, this cosmic clustering in financial wealth that has happened since the early 1980s shows no signs of curtailment. In 2001, some ninety-seven percent of all families *still* held no bonds. Families having stock holdings rose somewhat to more than half, but not necessarily to the lasting benefit of those people. Those in the bottom fifth of household income now had a median $7000 in holdings, but those in the top ten percent of income held a median value of $247,700, with half of those families having more. The median value of stock holdings of this upper tenth in 2001 was three point six times the median of the year 1995. The overall wealth equality has worsened over time. With more detailed data on household wealth, we find the median net worth of the twenty-fifth percentile increasing only slightly, from $1600 to $2000 between the Orwellian year of 1984 and 1999, while the top five percent enjoyed a sixty-one point two four percent gain, from $483,120 to $799,000.

When national and even global policies are aimed at, first, inflating, then, pumping new air into asset bubbles, we should not be surprised that working people are left behind. The Wall Street-Greenspan financial markets strategy led to financial asset inflation. Greenspan's decision to be the cheerleader for the New Economy and outrageously high stock prices inflated the bubbles still more. The Goldilocks Economy kept the bubbles in animated suspension even as it kept wages and benefits of workers soft. International competition from low wages (and corporate threats to move jobs offshore in an environment of weak labor unions and low minimum wages) held wages and benefits down in the U.S.

TOLES © (2005) The Washington Post. Reprinted with permission of UNIVERSAL PRESS SYNDICATE. All rights reserved.

The Continuing Problem with Wall Street and Greenspan's Financial Markets Strategy

The legacy of Wall Street and Greenspan lives on. The wealth holders in the bond market to this day deeply fear strong economic growth; the wealth holders in the stock market still fear what the Fed might do to slow things down. So, we appear stuck with a great economic paradox that began during the mid-1990s: Economic indicators behaving badly for the working class are good for securities whereas good economic news for the workers lead to a bear market. The concerns of the typical family correctly are, however, not so much with the fears of the financial wealth holders, but with the ramifications of those fears for itself. Since the Reserve has given full employment a bad name, the rich will resist any temptation to place their funds into productive capital such as plant and equipment whose idleness has become a good omen. Alan Greenspan and the Reserve have heightened the danger associated with good news for the working class that also is bad news for the financial markets. When calming reassurance oozes from wizard Alan Greenspan or other Fed chairs, it is the opiate of the financial wealth holding class.

11

GLOBAL MARKET FAILURES

*Surely, one might have argued, there must be some basis for their
[International Monetary Fund and U.S. Treasury] position,
beyond serving the naked self-interest of financial markets, which saw
capital market liberalization as just another form of market
access—more markets in which to make more money.*

Joseph E. Stiglitz, *Globalization and Its Discontents*
(New York/London: W.W. Norton, 2002) Stiglitz,
2001 Nobel Prize winner in Economics, is writing of the
East Asian crisis of 1997–1998. He was chief economist
and senior vice president of the World Bank at the time.

Much of the language of international finance has become as tainted as
speech at central banks. "Liberalization" and "transparency" of financial markets has been pushed by the United States as well as the World
Bank and International Monetary Fund that it dominates. The freeing of capital markets in such unlikely places as Russia and Indonesia is
"liberal" by the nineteenth century European meaning of the term. It is
laissez faire extended to markets that cry out for the need of judicious
regulation. What moves most freely really are money flows because
computers enable banks and other financial institutions to instanta-
neously move liquid assets from an account in New York City to an
account in Istanbul. Wall Street praises such free-flowing arrangements
as efficient markets at work, as did Alan Greenspan and Robert Rubin.
But, if it is only money, not real capital that flows in one of its myriad
forms, the only gain is for its lucky recipient.

The Asian Crises, 1997–1998

Alan Greenspan was holding the fed funds rate steady but above five percent; it was a policy presumably directed at a goods inflation that was more imaginary than real. American workers began to make some gains that were unwelcome on Wall Street. Amid signs of modest wage gains for the first time in nearly a quarter century, Wall Street was looking beyond U.S. borders for "good news." Japan, as well as Malaysia, South Korea, Indonesia, Thailand, and the Philippines—burdened with industrial overcapacity, ominous real estate bubbles, and failing banks—were beginning to have an adverse effect on U.S. manufacturing growth. Some economists were forecasting a substantial reduction of the U.S. GDP growth rate. Normally, for Wall Street and the Fed, this would be "good news."

Alan Greenspan and the Street, however, had not counted on financial markets misbehaving in Asia and possibly spilling over into the United States, despite their having extended liberalization of finance to southeastern Asia. When the Hong Kong stock market crashed on October 27, 1997, however, it triggered a global financial jolt that included a record breaking 550-point one-day drop in the Dow. Global financial markets were now fed by financial multinationals that would include Wall Street's largest banks. The drop in the Dow was temporarily bad news for the American wealth holders. Now, however, a slowdown in U.S. GDP growth would ease the perceived pressures in the labor markets for employment and higher wages. Promises of a growth slowdown had come, in the Street's view, just in time. This was *really* "good news."

Some bumps on the gold-bricked road nonetheless loomed ahead. The Asian crisis had yet to slow immoderate consumption in the United States, much of which slipped over into foreign markets. The nation's unemployment rate, at four point two percent in May 1998, was the lowest measured since 1970. Yet inflation reflected price stability for everyone except paranoid central bankers. It was a conundrum before Greenspan had used the term.

The maestro still seemed not quite satisfied, but was conciliatory. He told the Joint Economic Committee of Congress on June 10, "We at the Federal Reserve . . . have not perceived to date the need to tighten policy." In response, Wall Street breathed a short-lived sigh of relief. The Dow Jones industrial index climbed nearly 60 points from its level at the start of Greenspan's three-hour appearance. (Greenspan monitored the financial markets as he spoke before Congress.) But the market plunged in the final two hours of trading, apparently not sufficiently reassured by Greenspan's comments. "There is a bias toward restraint but . . . don't look for a tightening move imminently," confided a Fed Watcher in Chicago, one of many translators of Greenspanspeak. "He is saying . . . 'I will do the right thing when inflation threatens, but it is not threatening right now'." Despite such reassurances from trusted observers, the anxiety was palpable.

Uncharacteristically, a decade after the 1987 crash, contrary movements in bond and stock prices again began to happen. As the Asian crisis began to cut into U.S. corporate profits by summer 1998, bonds began to rally. When enough dark clouds hang over the economy, declining profits can turn the Goldilocks's Economy into recession at the expense of stock prices, as happened after the Crash of 1929. The Goldilocks Economy really must be "*just right*." The collapse of the Asian economies was *good* insofar as it slowed the American economy enough to end the modest growth in workers' wages. However, if the U.S. economy languished, the Asian depression and its domino effects would provide *too much* of a good thing. The balance by midsummer 1998 could not have been more precarious, nor more menacing, if not for the financial wealth holding class, for ordinary Americans. Once again, concerns were shifting to the failure of entire markets. The next market failure would be in the United States but would threaten a global financial system already under siege.

In early September 1998 another financial crisis loomed, requiring immediate attention. Then, when Greenspan merely hinted that he was as likely to *lower* as to raise interest rates, the Dow made its largest point rise ever, a 380-point leap in one day. If anything, the influence of the wealth holders had heightened as the Dow has swung wildly— hundreds of points from week to week, sometimes from day to day, sometimes *within* the day.

Market Failure at Long-Term Capital Management Turns Global

Hedge funds, a relatively new institution of the casino economy, essentially answer to no oversight institution, either state or federal, even though the funds make speculative, multibillion dollar bets with borrowed money in liberalized markets around the world. Among other laws, hedge funds can operate under a neat little 1996 amendment to U.S. securities laws that exempt from regulation funds limited to fewer than 500 "sophisticated" institutions or individuals—those that invest more than $25 million or $5 million, respectively. Ordinary, unsophisticated persons must put funds in tightly-regulated mutual funds that have high fees, commissions, and other restrictions.

One of the first of the hedge funds and the one considered the "best" was Long-Term Capital Management (LTCM). More exclusive than most, the minimum amount that LTCM would accept from those "sophisticated" wealth holders was $10 million. It had the rocket

OLIPHANT © (1999) UNIVERSAL PRESS SYNDICATE. Reprinted with permission. All rights reserved.

scientists who not only wrote the book on derivatives but shared a 1997 Nobel Prize in economics for writing it—LTCM partners Myron Scholes and Robert Merton. Its brain trust also included insider David Mullins Jr., former vice chairman of the Federal Reserve Board. The hedge fund was founded by a former vice chairman of Salomon Brothers Inc., John Meriwether. While Mullins was at the Fed, Meriwether was one of the "Masters of the Universe" dealing in bonds in the 1980s at renowned investment bank Salomon. Meriwether's career was disrupted in 1991 when he resigned in the midst of a Treasury-bond bid-rigging scandal. In Mullins view at the time, trying to corner the Treasury bond market was not sufficient reason to impose new regulations on bond underwriters, especially the Fed's primary dealers. LTCM could easily have been mistaken for a branch bank of the Fed somewhere in up-state New York.

Greenspan Arranges a Bailout of LTCM's Lenders to "Save" the Global Financial System

Despite having doubled its money from 1994 to 1997, LTCM essentially was bankrupt by September 1, 1998. Not to worry, Alan Greenspan and other officials considered Long-Term Capital, if not too big to fail, too big with former Fed officials and too big on the balance sheets of Merrill Lynch, Goldman Sachs, J.P. Morgan, and other friendly financial giants to be allowed to fail. Moreover, these balance sheets extended to subsidiaries and financial alliances around the globe. At about $80 billion in debt, not only did LTCM owe more money than most nations, it had more than a *trillion* dollars of complex derivative contracts with these banks, brokerage houses, and others.

On September 23, 1998 Greenspan was busily arranging the last-minute rescue of LTCM. As it teetered on collapse, executives from Wall Street's largest brokerages, investment banks and commercial banks held round-the-clock meetings with Fed officials. With Greenspan's blessing, then New York Fed president William McDonough put the chieftains of Merrill Lynch, Travelers Group, Salomon Smith Barney, Goldman Sachs, Credit Suisse First Boston, and others on the 10th floor of the bank, twisted a few arms, and brokered the bailout of what was, essentially, a partnership of high-tech gamblers. Not since J.P. Morgan had huddled with the other bulky bankers of his day during the Great Crash of 1929, had so many financiers come to such quick agreement.

No one giant could resist McDonough's arm-twisting because, they knew, if they did not cooperate, they could not count on the Reserve when they needed help, which happened to be now. It was the same technique used by E. Gerald Corrigan, McDonough's predecessor at the N.Y. Fed, to maintain global liquidity after the stock market crash of 1987. As to LTCM, it had received a faxed offer earlier in the day from a group consisting of Warren Buffett, Goldman Sachs and American International Group. Buffet, *et al.* offered to buy out the fund's contributors for $250 million, and to put another $3.75 billion into the fund's capital. The managers would be fired. The Federal Reserve came through with a better offer for the contributors *and* the managers who were not only retained but given a fee to be paid by the contributors to the bailout.

Again, the hypocrisy, even if it is innocent, is too obvious to ignore. Just ten days before the bailout, Greenspan had told a Congressional hearing why *regulation* of hedge funds is *unnecessary*: "Hedge funds are strongly regulated by those who lend the money," he explained, "they are not technically regulated in the sense that banks are, but they are under fairly significant degree of surveillance." Despite the "technically *un*regulated" nature of such hedge funds, Greenspan and the New York Fed convened the heavyweights of Wall Street to raise $3.65 billion within 24 hours. Ironically, on the *same day* of the bailout, the Federal Reserve Board was approving the merger of Citicorp and Travelers Group Inc. (one of Long-Term's creditors), creating the world's largest financial-services company—at $750 billion, also definitely "too big to fail." Since almost every major Wall Street securities firm and commercial bank had lent enormous sums to LTCM, its collapse could have forced a fire sale of securities and shaken confidence in an already fragile global financial system, bringing down some Wall Street giants with it. Rather than LTCM itself, these giant Wall Street banks and brokerage houses themselves were bailed out (once again).

The giant hedge fund's losses came on the heels of Russia's default of debt. Greenspan defended the LTCM bailout before the House Banking Committee on October 1, 1998:

> Had the failure of LTCM triggered the seizing up of markets, substantial damage could have been inflicted on many market participants, including some not directly involved with the firm, and could have potentially impaired the economies of many nations, including our own. ...

He went on to suggest that LTCM would have been an insignificant event in calmer global markets. In short, what happened to LTCM was not its fault; Greenspan had lost no confidence in hedge funds, derivatives or The Market. The maestro promptly resumed his defense of unregulated hedge funds and derivatives markets.

When asked about the "bailout," then Treasury Secretary Rubin testily replied, "That wasn't a bailout . . . What the Federal Reserve Bank of New York did was to convene [a meeting]. These creditors made their own private-sector decisions." Still, the twisting of arms by McDonough could be heard as far away as the Trinity Church graveyard. With the global financial system hanging in the balance, the Federal Reserve had to use either the private creditors' funds or its own in the rescue. If the private creditors would have voluntarily bailed out Long-Term Capital, why did the Fed believe a meeting was necessary?

The financial wealth holders welcomed the news of the bailout. It eased fears of a wholesale liquidation of the LTCM's bond portfolio. For a while at least, the bailout, together with Greenspan's immediate interest rate reduction helped the tone of the overall bond market. The bailout also raised the possibility that the Fed would have to be that much more accommodative on interest rates and credit; Greenspan seemed to be promising as much in congressional testimony the day of the bailout. Bond holders, at least, could sleep a little better at night.

Global finance began to resemble Baskin-Robbins Ice Cream; there was a new flavor of financial market failure of every month. Early in October 1998, the U.S. dollar endured its biggest two-day drop in a quarter century as panic selling swept the world's $1.5 trillion-a-day currency markets. This free fall was blamed in large part on hedge funds such as LTCM that had been betting on the dollar. Since LTCM was one of the "smaller" and "better" of the hedge funds, there are other minefields are out there. The subsequent quietness in the hedge fund field was deceptive. After all, none will reveal what is on their balance sheets while Alan Greenspan doesn't want to know.

Meanwhile, the revolving door of finance just keeps on spinning. When Corrigan left the New York Fed, he went to Goldman Sachs, one of the firms bailed out in the LTCM deal, and serves as a managing director. He chairs the Counterparty Risk Management Group II, a revival of a group formed in 1999, following the implosion of LTCM, to consider systemic risks in the financial system. It was reconvened in 2005 as newly serious concerns with hedge funds and derivatives began to resurface—to which we will return. Bill McDonough, retired from the Fed and named chairman of the Public Company Accounting Oversight Board, now worries that Americans' negative attitudes toward wealthy CEOs will lead to "more regulation." Robert Rubin completed his tour of bond duty by spinning out of the U.S. Treasury to become co-director of Citigroup, the mega-bank formed from the merger approved by Greenspan the day LTCM was bailed out. When Citigroup was required to pay a large fine in 2005 because of its duplicity in underwriting Enron, Rubin did not hesitate in calling President George W.'s Secretary of Treasury for relief. The Bush people never returned the phone call, perhaps because Rubin is not a Republican.

The U.S. International Deficit: It Just Keeps Getting Bigger and Bigger

The U.S. current-account deficit in its international balance of payments is mostly a trade deficit—the value of U.S. imports greatly exceeding its exports. This international deficit is of much greater duration than a bubble here and a bubble there, but still closely related to Wall Street and Alan Greenspan's financial markets strategy. The slow and halting economic growth of the Goldilocks Economy has put great downward pressures on U.S. wage rates. Deregulation combined with mass mergers of private commercial banks has created a surge in easy credit (through high-interest credit cards and low-interest equity loans to "clean up" that credit card debt) for wage earners, those who most need credit but can least afford it.

The marriage of low wages and credit cards has necessitated bargain hunting by typical American families in low-cost manufacturing countries such as China (marketed through Wal-Mart). China also has enjoyed a favorable exchange rate relative to the dollar, making its goods even cheaper for Americans. Not surprisingly, the more recent acceleration in the U.S. current account deficit is associated with the huge trade imbalance with China. The 2005 pegging of the Chinese yuan to a basket of currencies and its upward valuation by about two percent will have no effect on the trade balance but potentially speculative effects on capital flows into China, as speculators anticipate a slowly rising yuan.

Since Americans have been importing more goods than they have been exporting, this trade deficit must be funded by foreigners lending to the U.S. (by buying U.S. government bonds) or buying U.S. corporate equities and bonds. If we ignore little things like political risks, lower U.S. interest rates are less attractive to foreign lenders but more attractive for foreigners buying U.S. equities and higher U.S. interest rates are more attractive for buying U.S. bonds but less attractive for buying U.S. equities. By early August 2005, the fed funds rate was three point five percent in the U.S., the European central bank rate was two percent, and interest rates in Japan were near zero. The buyers of U.S. government bonds include foreign central banks that need the dollars to stabilize the international values of their own currencies.

Embedded in the capital inflows, which comprise about six point five percent of the U.S. GDP, is a troubling paradox. Poor countries, mostly in Asia, are financing consumption in a very rich country. Plain old economics says that rich countries should be exporting funds to fast-growing poor Asian nations. Why has plain vanilla economics been turned upside down? Think of it this way: rich people and institutions in otherwise poor nations can achieve saver returns by lending to Americans. Rich Americans feel the same way. This awkward paradox can be sustained only as long as American wage earners are willing to borrow and buy Asian goods at low prices and Middle Eastern oil at rising prices.

Blowing Bubbles

By 2005, the risks to the global economy were beginning to match those going into the end of the 1990s. The U.S. current-account deficit was accelerating between 1998 and the recession beginning in the year 2000 (during which it slowed). The ever-widening deficit rose from around four percent of GDP going into the year 2000 to that six point five percent in 2005. Instead of high bond yields, the world was enjoying remarkably low bond yields (despite ten fed funds rate increases, admittedly "measured," by early August). Sometimes the Fed worries about these foreigners cashing out of their holdings of U.S. bonds and stocks. That could cause our financial markets to collapse. Although a lax regulatory environment had greatly contributed to the earlier market failures, the regulatory environment in the U.S. and around the world had virtually disappeared by the year 2005.

Despite the loss-loss records of the Federal Reserve, Alan Greenspan continues to prefer a "hands-off approach" when it comes to bubbles or other market failures (which he denies can happen) and simply clean up the mess afterward. The European Central Bank attempts to prevent the bubbles in the first place. Ironically, the new environment had been created by the Fed's efforts to "clean up" the mess that it had greatly contributed to during the 1980s and especially after the mid-1990s. At least the new mess that Greenspan has created is different (mess diversification?), but in many respects potentially more dangerous. In proper order, we move on to the new asset bubbles crafted by Greenspan and company.

12

THE COLLAPSE OF
THE GREAT AMERICAN
STOCK MARKET BUBBLE

POINT: But how do we know when irrational exuberance has unduly escalated asset values, which then become subject to unexpected and prolonged contractions as they have in Japan over the past decade?

COUNTERPOINT: We as central bankers need not be concerned if a collapsing financial asset bubble does not threaten to impair the real economy, its production, jobs, and price stability. Indeed, the sharp stock market break of 1987 had few negative consequences for the economy.

Alan Greenspan in his famous "irrational exuberance" speech, "The Challenge of Central Banking in a Democratic Society," at the Washington Hilton, sponsored by the conservative American Enterprise Institute for Public Policy Research, December 5, 1996.

It was far from obvious that bubbles, even if identified early, could be pre-empted short of the central bank inducing a substantial contraction in economic activity—the very outcome we would be seeking to avoid.

Alan Greenspan in an August 2002 speech at an annual Federal Reserve conference in Jackson Hole, Wyoming.

Greenspan went on to accelerate deregulation of banking and financial markets, at home and abroad. Yet, rising financial fragility was crying out for the kinds of financial regulations inimical to an Ayn Rand, an Alan Greenspan or a neoconservative. It was a Faustian bargain for the maestro; ultimately he would have to deal with the manias, as he had done before. First, the Fed would abdicate control of the financial markets once the wealth holders became irrational speculators. Then, the demons they unleashed would take on lives of their own. "Risk management" would continue to be Greenspan's mantra.

Goldilocks: Prelude to Irrational Exuberance

Before we move on to the market reactions to Greenspan's most famous speech, there is irony or truth, depending on whose side we are on, in what Greenspan had done the July before. The Dow, after more than doubling in less than two years, dived more than three point five percent on July 12, 1996. Chairman Greenspan had yet to speak, but had no choice since he was scheduled to testify on July 18 at his then-mandated semiannual Humphrey-Hawkins report on monetary policy. With considerable practice by this time, the financial wealth holders were easily able to hold their collective breaths. Wall Street pundits expected Greenspan to soothe the nerves of shareholders by carefully avoiding any strong hints of future interest rate increases. The maestro did not disappoint; he proceeded to blow smoke for about three hours. Well, he did more than that. He recited a litany of Goldilocks Economy blessings.

"Now, listen up, gather round," as the more charismatic "music man" from River City, Iowa would have put it. The maestro had "good news" for the marching band of Good News Bears. Energy prices were declining and an expected "budget-deficit reduction" would lead to low interest rates and a healthy credit market. And, luckily, the economy was about to slow: "Looking forward, there are a number of reasons to expect demands to moderate and economic activity to settle back toward a more sustainable pace in the months ahead." Better still, "The governors and [Fed] bank presidents ... view the prospects for inflation to be more favorable going forward." To top it off, the Fed was determined "to hold the line on inflation." With a capital "T" and that rhymes with "P" and that stands for prices; not only would the U.S. enjoy price stability but the maestro was going to keep it that way. What was good "for the economy" was mighty good for the financial wealth holders: "Because workers are more worried about their own job security and their marketability if forced to change jobs, they are apparently accepting smaller increases in their compensation at any given level of job market tightness."

The Coming of Irrational Exuberance

We note several things about Alan Greenspan's most famous speech. In typical Greenspanspeak, the maestro made two contradictory points about stock prices: (1) they are too high and (2) the Fed should not be concerned. Though he later denied the importance of his term "irrational exuberance," he knew perfectly well that his comments would have an adverse, if temporary, effect on stock prices. Only two days earlier, Greenspan had met privately with key people on Wall Street to warn them about "overvalued" stock prices. This advance notice to the financial wealth holders quickly filtered through the tight-knit investment banking community; they not only took heed, but profits and the Dow suffered its largest decline in four months. No blue collar workers or officers of labor unions had been invited to the meeting with Wall Street insiders.

Greenspan was "talking" to a market that he otherwise considers "perfect," attempting to browbeat stock prices down instead of using the blunter force of interest rate increases to slow speculation. An interest rate hike would have been an act defying deniability. Put differently, Greenspan was determined that any stock market debacle would not be the "Greenspan Crash of 1996." This must have been an awkward and painful moment for Greenspan, who trusts (only) himself to make the necessary course corrections in The Market.

True to Greenspan's instincts, within twenty-five minutes of his evening speech, U.S. stock market futures began to take a beating. On the other side of the world, Australia, Tokyo, and Hong Kong's markets plunged two to three percent. Germany followed with a roughly four percent drop for the day. When the price contagion reached American shores, U.S. stocks dropped by about two percent, but the Dow rallied in the afternoon with an announcement of the unemployment rate climbing slightly to five point four percent (good news for the Good News Bears). The Dow still slipped 200 points for the week.

Behind the Curtain

We did not know this at the time, but transcripts of Fed meetings released years later gives Greenspan, now the oracle, transparency. As early as spring 1994, a full two years and two seasons before his "irrational exuberance" speech, he was worrying that a stock-market bubble was forming. It was. In an effort to partly to let some air out, he did raise interest rates, to effects that proved temporary. At the time Greenspan *publicly denied* that stock market prices were playing a role in directing his actions. In this he was again being transparently opaque; the wizard was simply using invisible inflationary expectations in goods prices, a condition Wall Street loves to hate, as a reason for temporizing out-of-control financial speculation.

Wall Street envisioned rising interest rates cooling an economy that, while not running hot, was too warm for old-fashioned comfort. By now the financial wealth holders understood the benefits from an *economy lacking exuberance*. The financial wealth holders, now conditioned to the merits of a Goldilocks Economy, prematurely concluded that the Fed had successfully achieved a *soft landing* for the economy. To repeat, the wealth holders did not know that what Greenspan was saying in Federal Open Market Committee meetings was different, as in "wholly contrary to what he was saying publicly." They did not know at the time that he was concerned that stock prices were rising too fast. It was a concern that the wizard would soon renounce for long-held ideological and thus predictable reasons.

Bubble Fears at the Fed

Greenspan was not the only Governor at the Fed concerned with a possible stock market bubble. As the Dow approached 6000 in fall 1996, Lawrence Lindsey told Mr. Greenspan and fellow governors that the Fed should halt the bull market. "All bubbles end badly," Mr. Lindsey warned. Despite concerns within the Fed and despite the "irrational exuberance" speech, the Dow soared to 9000 by spring 1998 and pressures mounted for Mr. Greenspan to do something—to take action—rather than just talking about a possible bubble.

Mr. Lindsey recalls the discussions during the FOMC meeting with Dr. Greenspan in which he contends that aggressive action by the Fed *after* the crash could have prevented the Great Depression. To some degree Greenspan is correct when he says, as Lindsey recalls it, "1929 didn't cause 1932. It depends on what you do in 1930 and 1931." A possible interpretation: the Fed could have allowed the market to crash and then turned the economy around by great infusions of financial liquidity, providing enormous amounts of short-term loans to major financial institutions and reducing short-term interest rates. Since many other, much more important forces, caused the Great Depression, Greenspan's "thinking" is seriously flawed. The Fed contributed to the Great Depression by raising interest rates *too late* to prick the bubble but sufficiently early to contribute to the onset of the depression.

The Great End-of-Millennium Market Failures Compound the Errors

As noted, Greenspan has overseen many market failures; by the end of summer 1998 they were cascading on top of each other. The currency crisis in Southeastern Asia had thrown Indonesia, Malaysia, Singapore, and Thailand into severe economic contractions. The collapse of the Brazilian currency was having a similar effect in Latin America. Japan and Russia were mired in depression. Europe was preoccupied with monetary union and an economic slowdown. On Wall Street a giant hedge fund, Long-Term Capital Management, had to be bailed out by the Reserve.

All of these events threatened the on-going bull market in securities. After holding his trigger finger off the fed funds rate for a year and a half, Greenspan shot the fed funds rate down by a quarter percentage point on September 29, 1998 in reaction to the foreign currency and financial market crises. Then, on October 15 came another cut in reaction to the LTCM collapse; the rate settled at four point seven five percent, the lowest in four years. Foreign stock markets began to stabilize. The Fed had shifted fully to a goal of risk management, which, as Greenspan has noted, is not a legislated responsibility. Neither has the U.S. Congress mandated that the Reserve create financial bubbles.

With these rate cuts, the attention of the financial wealth holders shifted from the Dow to the Nasdaq. The Nasdaq, the favored market for initial public offerings (IPOs) of Internet and tech stocks, is analogous to the Times Industrials index of the Jazz Age, which had the "hi-techs" of the times—radio, television, auto and airline stocks. However, even the stodgy Dow went from 2500 in 1990 to 11,000 by the year 2000, after taking it a hundred years to reach 1000 in 1982. The Nasdaq, at a modest 300 in 1990 had gone to about 1000 in 1996 (the year of irrational exuberance), but had soared to 5049 by early March 2000.

Not only did Greenspan have a lot to do with it, Wall Street loved what he was doing. By successfully crusading for non-intervention by others, by pushing for the extension of American multilateral banks such as Citicorp (later, Citigroup) into foreign markets, by plumbing for "free markets" in Russia, by engineering the Goldilocks Economy, by bailing out failing banks and hedge funds, Greenspan became the leader of the casino economy, at home and abroad. The maestro could do no wrong. He had single-handedly purged that great demon, goods inflation, or so it was thought, and, better, he was busily inflating bonds and stocks.

Wall Street, by now in awe of Greenspan, still was marveling at Greenspan's interest rate cutting performance. When the markets merely shrugged as the Fed trimmed just a quarter percentage point off the fed funds rate, Greenspan immediately realized his error and followed up two weeks later with another quarter-percentage cut, without even calling a meeting of the Federal Open Market Committee. It was like a Pope taking dramatic actions without consulting his Cardinals.

Financial markets rallied instantly: bonds and stocks leapt. On November 17, 1998, David Wessel, a Staff Reporter of the *Wall Street Journal*, gushed about how Greenspan "knew the move would grab attention: it was the first time since 1994 that the central bank had changed interest rates between scheduled policy-committee meetings." Greenspan cut interest rates three times over the seven weeks between September 29 and Wessel's article. This time, the Reserve said, it wanted to reassure financial markets that it was prepared to do what was needed to avoid a global economic meltdown. The Reserve was acting as the global economy's central bank.

As to Greenspan's thinking, the truth was a bit murkier. Using an obscure measure, he concluded that liquidity in the bond market, especially for risky issues such as junk bonds, could dry up. That is, Greenspan was concerned that buyers of bonds were no longer willing to take great risks! To the immense relief of the Street, money was flowing back into corporate junk bonds from the high, safe ground of Treasuries after the cuts in the fed funds rate. Alan Greenspan's status as the Pope of Wall Street was assured.

Throughout this period Greenspan had a great deal of help from U.S. Treasury officials—especially his soul mate, then Treasury Secretary Robert Rubin. Though he barely needed them, Rubin had earned his wings as Wall Street's angel with a strong international dollar policy that had kept inflation low and had provided a cushion for the Federal Reserve to lower interest rates. A strong dollar, of course, made U.S. exports more expensive overseas and has contributed to historically massive trade deficits and downward pressures on American wages and full-time jobs, helping to wangle the Goldilocks Economy. Even after Rubin departed, the Wall Street-Greenspan financial markets strategy remained intact.

The Internet: The Bubble in the Bubble

As noted earlier, Alan Greenspan's expressed goal in Little Rock (before Clinton had stepped into the White House) *was* the achievement of a bull market in financial markets through a balanced federal budget and a zero inflation rate. Armed with his financial markets strategy, Greenspan had created hyperinflation in financial assets and contributed to a near-zero U.S. consumer inflation rate. With the three quick cuts in the fed funds rate ending in November 1998, wild movements in bond and stock prices resumed, and speculation in newly-minted Internet stocks created a bubble within a bubble. The anxiety of officials inside the Reserve intensified as the great financial bubble ballooned. Would Greenspan have to act?

Well, he didn't. Early in 1999, someone at the Ayn Rand Institute must have reminded Greenspan what he had always believed—that free market outcomes are always right. In defense of the Internet stocks,

Greenspan told the Senate Budget Committee on January 28, "the size of that potential market is so huge that you have these pie-in-the-sky type of potentials for a lot of different vehicles." Mr. Greenspan attributed the rise of Internet stocks to what he called "the lottery principle," under which people are willing to spend seemingly irrational sums of money in the hope they will hit the jackpot. He went on blithely:

> But there is at root here something far more fundamental. And indeed, it does reflect something good about the way our securities markets work; namely, that they do endeavor to ferret out the better opportunities and put capital into various different types of endeavors, prior to earnings actually materializing. That's good for our system. And that in fact—with all of its hype and craziness—is something that . . . probably is more plus than minus.

"Craziness?" Amazon.com, Yahoo!, eBay, and America Online took giant leaps upward that same day. Around mid-March, 1999, Yahoo!, the online directory service, was $175 a share, up from a year earlier price of only $16. America Online (AOL) went from the same price to $105. Meanwhile, the Dow broke through the psychological barrier of 10,000. By now, the Reserve's chair had, in quick succession, set off two rallies inside a speculative bubble of his own creation. Once fretting about "irrational exuberance," Greenspan now saw "craziness" in the financial markets as not only rational, but "good." People placing bets on companies with no earnings is what capitalism is all about! Willie Nelson wrote the song, Patsy Cline famously recorded it, but it was Alan Greenspan, once a clarinetist, romancing the financial markets. He had made the financial casino a hit.

Red flags were flying all over the Federal Reserve by now. In May, the Fed's staff warned at an FOMC meeting that rising stock prices were creating a bubble that threatened to create economic instability. Donald Kohn, than a top Fed staffer and later a Fed governor, suggested several policy options. One was to raise interest rates promptly if the committee thought that the eventual collapse of the stock bubble posed a sufficient threat to the health of the economy and the financial system. Mr. Greenspan had a contrary view. He told the members he didn't want to be the prick of the bubble (though he phrased it differently). For one thing, it was hard to second-guess millions of investors on the right value for stock prices. For another, deflating a bubble bigger than the *Outback* blimp would require interest rates so high they'd also shipwreck the economy.

A Bedeviling Aftermath

As the demons took over The Market, the bubble began to deflate all by itself in April 2000. It was the start of a slow-moving but nonetheless devastating meltdown. Greenspan, after giving the early, even premature warning, either postponed action too long or thought that the economy could be cleaned up later (based on his wrong earlier appraisal or what would have *failed* during the Great Depression). That is, Greenspan kept his faith in The Market; he decided to ride the run-up in the stock market prices. His pricking the bubble would not only have prevented the wealthy from becoming wealthier but also would have damaged Greenspan's legacy.

Then, after the tragic September 11, 2001 attacks on the World Trade Center in New York City, the Fed cut rates four more times, and did so again in 2002 after corporate scandals in an under-regulated environment had undermined investor confidence. Then, in 2003, with Iraq and the threat of *deflation* and another Great Depression hanging over the economy, the Fed cut rates again. By June 2003, the federal funds rate was at one percent, the lowest in almost a half-century.

Ultimately, even Alan Greenspan had to come to grips with the effects of mass hysteria. A "devil-may-care" behavior—manic, obsessed, haunted, mesmerized, and orgasmic—leads to abnormal outcomes. When the wealth holders overdo it, the mania must somehow end, usually an atrabilious end. The markets for securities or real estate—whatever the instrument of excess—eventually collapse and a credit crunch ensues. With a bubble imploding, with a weakening economy and the Great Depression as his guide, Mr. Greenspan cut the Fed funds rate sharply—twice in January 2001 and five times more through August. By the end of the year 2001 the rate cuts totaled eleven in the fastest credit-easing campaign in Federal Reserve history. Short-term interest rates reached forty-five-year lows. The new fear was goods prices *deflation*. Meanwhile, the speculative fever had moved out of Nasdaq and into hedge funds and real estate, with the Dow nonetheless beginning a bubble-like new rally. Did the demons move on to hedge funds, real estate and revisit the Dow?

13

DERIVATIVES: THROWING IN THE CHIPS

Greenspan and Wall Street's aspirations have created spiraling volatility in global financial markets. The greatly enhanced instability in security prices, not seen since the Jazz Age, has put the players at greater risk. Wealth holders, be they persons or banks, began to look anxiously for financial instruments that might lessen those risks. Wall Street willingly created derivatives or "chips" that, it claimed, would lessen this self-inflicted risk. Derivatives are as old as Tulip bulb futures, but in financial markets a derivative originally was an asset whose value "derives" from that of a plain vanilla security such a U.S. Treasury bond or shares of General Motors. While those derivatives are still around, the variety of new derivatives created on Wall Street has increased faster than the acumen of the traders. While the presence of notional or imaginary financial "assets" valued at a multiple of the real global economy is frightening, a plethora of derivatives has been moving the global financial casino toward completeness, a gambler's paradise.

At first blush, it seems odd that any players on Wall Street would welcome volatility. For most persons financial volatility leads to uncertainty and confusion. If we have funds in a 401 k or other savings program, we would like to believe that the chance of its falling in value by eighty percent is nil. In contrast to the small-time financial player, great volatility has great advantages for major speculators; it can lead to greater *potential* capital gains. Speculators love volatility even as they create it. And, so, with rising volatility in financial markets, the financial casino now goes beyond those in Las Vegas, Atlantic City or Monte Carlo because the only chips required are in the computers used for settling trades. The financial casino has invented simply numbers to be bought and sold—much like trading ether. Since nobody seems to care what they are, they can use *imaginary chips* to leverage the ordinary chips, a switch that began with what used to be a conservative financial instrument, bonds and their interest rates. The speculators are mostly wealthy persons, multinational banks and some new exotic players.

Today any commercial bank without interest-rate derivatives, which are held off its balance sheet, is considered "inefficient." Alan Greenspan, in particular, was the first policymaker to declare derivatives to be an instrument of market efficiency, which would make what he had already decided were perfect markets, somehow better. The perfect market became its own metaphor even as the contradiction became more blatant. On Wall Street, *every* new instrument is said to meet "a need in the marketplace." Wall Street's needful conjures images of *Les Misérables*—crippled orphans, aging widows, and homeless children—milling about the graveyard of the Trinity Church. Their palsied hands are reaching out for the solid nourishment derivable only from another mutated bond or for the liquid nourishment derivable only from an "asset" based on a debt backed by a second debt backed by a third debt and so on, to the bottom of the universe of stocks and bonds. The Wall Street broker's failure to meet a need in the marketplace is a sin punishable by purgatory in a place like Fargo or, upon second offense, a consignment to sell Italian shoes in Chinatown.

To describe this financial transformation is to reveal its dangers, the gravest of which is the entire financial casino closing. Still, to be fair to the very wealthy, if they are to speculate; they must not only have a goodly supply of chips but plenty of games to play. Takeovers by leveraged junk bonds initially provided not only red chips to go with the blue but some new games. Then, as bond speculation increased volatility, commercial bankers got into the game. Increasingly deregulated financial institutions became remarkably innovative in begetting new financial instruments in which bond proceeds and interest could be stored momentarily for quick appreciation or leveraged for still greater gains.

Deregulation: The All-intrusive Greenspan Becomes the Financial Czar

Deregulation in the financial industry—begun earnestly under Jimmy Carter, a *cause célèbre* under Ronald Reagan, heroically inspired by

Alan Greenspan—stimulated takeovers. By 1998 the ten largest banks, headed by Citigroup (formerly Citicorp) in New York, held more than a *third* of all commercial bank assets. After a flurry of mergers, the trillion-dollar bank was a given. Absurdly, the junk bonds (abetted by Greenspan in his private consultancy) that ravaged the S & L industry had temporarily reduced the need for banks, turning consolidation of private banks from a luxury into a necessity. Fortuitously, the S & L industry collapsed under the weight of junk and, later, Greenspan was to stage an amazing coup d'état.

The wizard's ultimate triumph (along with the banks) came in the Gramm-Leach-Bliley Act of 1999, which gave the Federal Reserve System an umbrella of regulatory power over all financial services in the United States. The bill was essentially written by members of the staff of the Federal Reserve Board under Chairman Greenspan's direction. The Act simultaneously undid virtually every safeguard against financial misbehavior legislated since the Great Depression. Against great political forces over time, Greenspan's legislative achievement would be remarkable even absent the irony. The Act gave Greenspan the regulatory authority to make American finance about as laissez faire as he desired! Since the Federal Reserve is independent in every conceivable sense, no president of the United States and no important member of the U.S. Congress dared mention the obvious: Greenspan was now the czar of American financial markets and by extension, those of much of the world.

Corporate junk-bond financing was eating into the banks' loan business by the mid-1980s. Selling bonds directly to the public became easier, thereby bypassing banks. What only the *Fortune 500* companies could do in the 1970s, now lower-quality corporate borrowers could emulate, by issuing junk bonds. Though this market slowed sharply after Michael Milken was indicted in 1989, it was rekindled, even to conflagration, in the 1990s. By the end of 1998, the telecommunications industry, which, given an explosive growth of the Internet and other digital services, was touted as having the "safest plays" in the junkyard. With Merrill Lynch's junk-bond index well above Treasuries, Margaret Patel, a portfolio manager, was advising, "even if you don't see a lot of capital appreciation in high yield, and all you do is earn the coupon, you can still do as well as you'll probably do in equities." Besides, junk bonds were increasingly viewed as "less risky" than those high-flying stocks.

Alan Greenspan and company did not want to leave commercial banks out of the lucrative junk business. After all, if junk was good enough for the S & Ls, it should be even better for banks. Thus, the Gramm-Leach-Bliley Act loosened restrictions to allow commercial banks to underwrite corporate securities, something outlawed since that Wild West practice had contributed to the Great Depression. Unleashed once more, commercial banks have muscled their way into the lucrative, but riskier junk-bond business. By the year 2005, Bank of America, J.P. Morgan and Citigroup had risen to the top of the underwriter ranks. This, it is said on Wall Street, is a natural extension of commercial or, really, now "universal" banking. These same banks have provided short-term loans to corporations that are buying out other firms. Now, in turn, the banks can lengthen the finance terms by underwriting the high-yield (junk) bonds of the buyout firm and peddling those to mostly wealthy clients. These junk-leveraged buy-outs (LBOs), once the exclusive province Mr. Milkin but then frowned upon by Wall Street banks as "highly speculative" or even illegal, are now enthusiastically embraced. Bank of America was underwriting junk bonds at an annual rate of $100 billion in the first half of 2005.

Why Do Commercial Bankers Swap Interest Rates Instead of Spouses?

Short answer: Spouses are less volatile. Of all bond prices and yields, junk bonds are the most volatile, an instability that infects other securities, making them more like insecurities. In a classic Catch-22, Alan Greenspan and the banking industry have embraced derivatives as devices used to cope with spiraling bond market volatility. Since banks hold and issue debt paying interest, they are exposed to the perils of interest-rate fluctuations on both sides of their balance sheets. But that has always been the case. Astonishingly volatile bond prices and interest rates—to which the Fed has greatly contributed—created the need to reduce rising risks. Unsurprisingly, the astounding growth in bank-related derivatives has been driven by contracts based on inter-est rates, the majority of which are in interest-rate swaps, said by the Reserve to be a "low-cost way for banks to manage their exposure to interest-rate fluctuations."

An *interest-rate swap* is pretty much like it sounds. An investment banker gets two bankers together—for a fee, of course—and one banker agrees to pay the interest it earns on *fixed*-rate assets to the second banker; in turn, the second banker agrees to pay the first banker the interest *he* receives on *variable*-interest assets. The swap can balance the values of assets and liabilities held by each bank in fixed interest and rate-sensitive interest instruments. However, only if the types of assets and liabilities are perfectly matched would a bank be completely free from interest-rate risk. Banks which speculate can intentionally or mistakenly maintain an imbalance between the values of like assets and liabilities.

It is worse; derivatives are not on the balance sheets of banks because, well, they are not balance-sheet items. I suppose that one day during the 1980s bankers got together and said: "Look, our balance-sheet assets and liabilities are highly volatile; the best way of reducing this volatility is to buy and sell contracts that *never appear on the bal-ance sheets*!" It was a brilliant idea, judging from the rapid growth in derivatives. Off-balance-sheet activities as a percentage of commercial banks' assets have doubled since 1979. Banks' holdings of off-balance-sheet derivatives stood at a notional, or an underlying, value of roughly $15.6 *trillion* in a more modest $6.7 trillion *real economy* at the end of 1994 and about twice the then value of the U.S. stock markets. The notional principal of outstanding exchange-traded and over-the-counter derivative contracts increased from less than $2 trillion at the end of 1986 to more than $20 *trillion* at the end of 1994, an average annual growth rate of one hundred and forty percent. (The notional principal amount is the number by which the interest rates or exchange rates in a derivative contract are multiplied to calculate the settlement amount.)

Most of these exotic ventures are conducted by a handful of dealer banks that specialize in such contracts. Only six banking corpora-tions, mostly in New York, control about eighty-five percent of the commercial banking derivatives' market. The replacement value of these derivatives was about $500 billion at the end of 1994, compared with less than forty percent of this value or $200 billion as the capital base of the 12 largest dealers. The replacement value is the unrealized capital gain or loss of the contract at current market prices. Besides interest-rate swaps, interest-rate futures, forward contracts, and options (plus various foreign exchange-rate contracts) comprise other derivatives of the banks. Stock market index futures and options comprise much of the balance of the derivatives' market.

Derivatives get complicated very fast. An entire book devoted to the subject could not hedge, as it were, all the possibilities. Since the dealers can differentiate their products by customizing derivatives, the possibilities are nearly endless. I am content to suggest two things; first, derivatives have become big business that banks and other institutions expect to continue to use and, second, things can go wrong with derivatives because they already have. Derivatives enable banks to leverage debt instruments and put ordinary customers' money at risk. The line between prudent hedging by a bank or other party and speculation is painfully long and thin. A central issue is whether a financial institution is entitled to issue or trade an enforceable gambling contract that would be illegal if anybody but a financial institution traded or wrote it. An interest-rate swap is a bet that interest rates will not go a particular direction, and is no different from a bet at a gaming table in Monte Carlo.

Greenspan Places His Trust in the Markets for Financial Derivatives

Alan Greenspan has taken an uncharacteristically clear position when he has talked about financial derivatives. In a speech in lovely Coral Gables, Florida on February 21, 1997, he urged a less cumbersome approach to regulating securities trading, especially derivatives and financial futures. "The less you interfere in the markets, the better," Greenspan said. "I've always believed that." Greenspan said he saw no need for regulating off-exchange derivative transactions, adding that the Commodity Exchange Act was an "inappropriate framework" for oversight of such trades. Financial innovations are to be encouraged because they increase the efficiency of financial markets. After all, what could be more reassuring than billions of complex wagers that are not even on the balance sheets? Greenspan nonetheless continues to hold his own wealth elsewhere.

The new financial derivatives became so important that they required a new financial institution to manage them—by the misnomer, hedge fund. Just as Greenspan (and others) told the S & L's that they could do anything they wanted, he has sent the same message to private banks and hedge funds. Besides, in other nations where the giant New York banks such as Bank of America and Citigroup deal, there is *no* official lender of last resort, unless the International Monetary Fund (IMF) takes on that responsibility. As the Indonesians discovered, the IMF is an unreliable ally. This leaves mostly the Fed and the U.S. government. As with the S & L bailout, the American taxpayer could end up picking up another very large tab at a time when the world needs a strong and reliable financial system.

If Alan Greenspan's legacy prevails, commercial (universal) banks will continue to be part of the problem rather than a way out. Greenspan's aggressively lax regulation spotlights the cozy relation of not only the Fed with Wall Street, but with the new institution of hedge funds. When the financial markets explode next time, can a Fed chair be trusted to do the right thing? Will the Fed do the right thing when and if a trillion-dollar bank collapses under the weight of junk bonds "hedged" by derivatives? With Greenspan having approved not only massive bank mergers but their underwriting and dealing securities, the new banks may be not only too large to save, but too compromised.

14

FED DEPENDENCE ON HEDGE FUNDS?

Hedge funds are strongly regulated by those who lend money. They are not technically regulated in the sense that banks are, but they are under a fairly significant degree of surveillance.

Alan Greenspan, as quoted by Anita Raghavan and Mitchell Pacell, "A Hedge Fund Falters, So the Fed Beseeches Big Banks to Ante Up," *Wall Street Journal*, September 24, 1998, p. 1. Greenspan made the statement ten days before the collapse of Long-Term Management Capital.

If, somehow, hedge funds were barred worldwide, the American financial system would lose the benefits conveyed by their efforts, including arbitraging price differentials away. The resulting loss in efficiency and contribution to financial value added and the nation's standard of living would be a high price to pay—to my mind, too high a price.

Alan Greenspan's Testimony, "Private-Sector Refinancing of the Large Hedge Fund, Long-Term Capital Management," Before the Committee on Banking and Financial Services, U.S. House of Representatives, October 1, 1998. After the collapse of LTCM, Greenspan is defending the use of the "good offices" of the Federal Reserve in convening of LTCM investors and lenders at the Federal Reserve Bank of New York.

What with the revival of the junk bond market by the mid-1990s and the ecumenical use of interest swaps by commercial banks, it was only a matter of time before junk bonds and derivatives would be combined in a newly unregulated financial institution. This wonderful invention, the *hedge fund*, would accept funds only from the super-rich, borrow money from the banks and brokerages it did business with, leverage those funds with interest swaps, and make money out of key strokes on its computer. In his October 1, 1998 testimony Greenspan effusively flattered LTCM as "a mutual fund that is structured to avoid regulation by limiting its clientele to a small number of highly sophisticated, very wealthy individuals..."

Though "hedge" used to denote the covering of risk, the hedge fund makes money speculating. Those banks and brokers lending to the hedge fund also put their own funds in it, which sounds like a conflict of "interest." The funds' play is not restricted to interest swaps, they can choose among several thousand derivatives. The funds are critical to the casino economy because at no time are hands dirtied by direct contact with crude oil, timber, pork bellies, steel, mining, manufacturing, or anything even remotely resembling real output. Nothing real is ever delivered.

These funds remain as secretive as Yale's Skull and Bones, which, according to member President George W. Bush, is too secret to talk about, making Skull and Bones almost as interesting as hedge funds. The mystery and glamour of hedge funds are exceeded only by their rapid growth. Their assets were estimated at about $1 trillion by 2005 (or about equal to the GDP of Canada), up from $400 billion in 2001. Even most of those who place their money or more accurately bets, in hedge funds can't get daily valuations, much less audited values. Wealthy individuals and giant institutions, the main players, do not seem to mind being kept in the dark as long as their names remain secret. These very private money pools can buy anything they want, from stocks and bonds to currencies and commodities. "Anything they want" includes those mysterious things *derived* from stocks, bonds, currencies, commodities, and other things—that is, derivatives.

The obscurity of such funds is assured by the kind of loose regulation worldwide championed by Alan Greenspan. As long as the funds cater to wealthy individuals and large institutions, Alan Greenspan and other market fundamentalists, consider hedge funds "safe" because the participants are "sophisticated." Apparently a perpetual pecuniary knowledge gap separates the wealthy from the poor and the middling class. The real mystery nonetheless is why wealthy individuals and giant institutions *voluntarily* take a vow of ignorance when they shift pieces of their wealth into hedge funds.

The Insides of a Hedge Fund

The collapse of Long-Term Capital Management (LTCM) gives us what we otherwise would not have—a look inside a hedge fund. LTCM specialized in bond arbitrage, whereby it placed complex and highly leveraged bets on the differences between interest rates on various kinds of bonds. Its core placements, based on complex computer models, were in the U.S., Japanese and the larger European markets. It was betting that the high interest rates on junk bonds would move toward or converge on fault-free U.S. Treasuries. By what Greenspan refers to as "arbitrage" by the hedge funds, they facilitate the convergence of interest rates of bonds of the same maturity to a single rate. With the Asian turmoil beginning in mid-1997 and culminating in the Russian political collapse and consequent financial problems in Latin America by autumn 1998, those holding riskier bonds dumped them—driving their yields upward—and bought U.S. Treasuries—driving their yields downward. Thus, interest rates, rather than converging, widened even more. LTCM had made its bets in the wrong direction. If markets are truly efficient, this convergence is supposed to take place automatically, without the need for hedge funds.

The game with bonds and chips was played this way. Suppose that five-year junk bonds historically have a yield four percentage points above five-year Treasuries because of their higher risk. The Scholes-Merton computer model, developed by the LTCM principals, might predict that when the yield differences widen to, say, six percentage points, the yields will converge back to only four percentage points. At a six percentage-point yield gap, Long-Term places a bet on the gap narrowing, agreeing to exchange the expected lower yield on $5 billion of junk bonds for the expected higher yield on $5 billion of Treasuries. This "interest rate swap" involves only a "notional" amount, the $5 billion, and, wonder of wonders, neither party owns the underlying securities, nor anything else, only the obligation to pay the differences in yields. From this bet grow the gambler's profits—unless, of course, as it happened, the bet is in the wrong direction! Though its contributors were not told about it, LTCM played the same game with price differences between merging companies.

Actually, LTCM's actions were more reckless than simply gambling. It was highly leveraged, having borrowed from Wall Street most of the funds it was putting on the table. At its peak, LTCM reportedly had a debt load *100 times* as great as its net assets, or ownership capital. This would be like putting down only $10,000 of your own money on a $1,000,000 house on a south Florida barrier island known to be in the direct path of a Category-5 hurricane (which, by the way, is now being done). Moreover, the fund had off-balance sheet derivative contracts valued "notionally" at $1.25 *trillion*. Alan Greenspan feared, belatedly but rightly, that further liquidation of LTCM's positions would weaken not only the bond markets of the troubled Asian, Russian, and Latin economies, but the U.S. financial markets as well, creating a panic. Still, he concluded, the barring of hedge funds, which never existed before sometime in the 1990s, would reduce the American standard of living. Which Americans?

Fast Forward to 2005: Hedge Funds Hit Main Street

Just before Memorial Day 2005 hedge funds were back in the business news. The long, but refreshing pause is no surprise, given the minimal public disclosure of the industry. Although invented to service the super-rich, a growing number of hedge funds now allow the modestly affluent to "go crazy" with their funds. The new funds are called "fund of funds," or mutual funds holding units in various hedge funds. The minimal requirement is $1.5 million in net worth or $200,000 income two years running. The minimum investment is $25,000. This shift in the marketplace from the super-rich to the modestly rich is commonplace.

The super-rich are path breakers when it comes to financial innovations. Once hedge fund assets approach a tenth of the American GDP, however, they begin to run out of risk-taking wealthy people and institutions, as well as unexploited profit opportunities. To regain or maintain profit margins, hedge funds must begin to market to those whose lesser wealth already assures that they are fiscally-challenged. Hedge funds for the modestly rich may not be as good an idea as the bad idea of hedge funds in the first place.

Suppose smaller players enter the hedge fund games in a big way. Such hedge fund members may also be sophisticatedly-challenged. Isn't this tantamount to allowing a barefooted golfer wearing a tee shirt—no soft spikes or Greg Norman golf shirt, much less a 528cc Taylor Made driver—to join an exclusive country club on Long Island? Perhaps that's why hedge funds returned to the front page of the *Wall Street Journal*, while the most famous golfer in Arkansas history and winner of two majors, John Daly, remained in the back pages.

Luckily, a few Republicans and some of the few Democrats still in public office worry about these "smaller players." In a spasm of conservative soul-searching at the Securities and Exchange Commission (SEC), its staff and outgoing director recommended that hedge funds register with the SEC effective in February 2006. Unfortunately, the SEC has virtually no rules that apply to them. Mandatory registration does not have the support of certain officials, including Alan Greenspan. Besides, thanks to Greenspan, the Fed is first among equals in "regulating" *all* financial institutions, including those under the SEC. Alan Greenspan has been crystal clear (though he also characteristically expressed some concerns in spring 2005): Hedge funds should go unregulated. Besides that, President W's new nominee to head the SEC, Representative Christopher Cox, as pro-free market as they come, may pull the plug on the pending rules changes. Even if he doesn't, the SEC's limited resources will likely prevent it from completing a review of a hedge fund before it has disappeared or changed its own rules.

Greenspan once again appears to be exceptional. Other regulators around the world, besides the SEC staff, are threatening to step up oversight of such funds. On June 23, 2005, the United Kingdom's financial-markets watchdog, the Financial Services Authority, warned that "some hedge funds are testing the boundaries of acceptable practice concerning insider trading and market manipulation." The Authority is particularly worried about the mega-managers who have billions of dollars in play. Hedge funds now account for an *estimated* thirty to forty percent of trading on Europe's largest stock market, the London Stock Exchange (no one knows the exact numbers). In Europe, German Chancellor Gerhard Schroder called for global regulation of hedge funds at a July 2005 summit meeting of the world's leading industrial nations.

Hedge Funds Get in Trouble in 2005

Since their invention, hedge funds have been associated with short-term trading of public securities and their derivatives, such as GM and Ford common stocks and options. We learned in 2005 that hedge funds also can "swap" payments obligations such as credit-default contracts as "insurance" against corporate defaults—such as on GM and Ford bonds. When GM and Ford bonds were unexpectedly downgraded in the spring, these trades went the wrong way for those hedge funds that did not *expect* anything to go wrong with GM and Ford bonds, only with their stocks. An offer by Kirk Kerkorian, the billionaire takeover artist, to buy five percent more equity in GM compounded difficulties; the price of GM stock rose while GM bonds were declared junk. Ford's bonds quickly turned to junk in abject sympathy. According to conservative estimates by Goldman Sachs the losses inflicted on hedge funds and large banks was about $1 billion.

More wrong bets could snowball. The International Swaps and Derivatives Association tells us that, at the end of 2004 the notional value of such swaps outstanding is $8.4 trillion, which about equals China's gross domestic product (GDP). Growing faster even than China, these swaps were up sixty-eight percent from the prior year. Still, the value of such credit derivatives is "small" next to the $183.6 trillion in interest-rate options and currency swaps also outstanding at the end of 2004, or five times the global annual GDP. The volume of derivatives relative to GDP reminds us of the power of the U.S. and Russian nuclear arsenals sufficient (still) to destroy the world several times. Eventually we will have sufficient derivatives to implode the world's financial markets several times.

These risks have mounted to the point that a group of financial-market vets led by no less than E. Gerald Corrigan, the former

New York Fed president and current managing director at Goldman Sachs Group, have reconvened. The revived Counterpart Risk Management Group II has been driven into action by the rise of hedge funds and the amazingly complex trading and risk-taking in financial markets. They released a timely report focused on the kind of credit markets that came unglued in spring 2005. Among other things, the report discusses how *illiquid* derivatives and other complex financial structures are priced. Are such price "quotes" real prices or merely hypothetical numbers? After all, the central problem of market failure is the disappearance of all semblance of a market. While a zero price for an imaginary number seems only fitting, the amounts of real money at risk can be staggering.

Hedge Funds Take on Bankers' Roles

If we want to find the power in the U.S., we need only follow the money; thus, we would expect a shift in power from Wall Street to Greenwich, Connecticut, where more than one hundred hedge funds reside. Ironically, at the end of a long chain of deregulatory moves, Alan Greenspan may have greatly altered the connections among the Fed and what used to be exclusively "bankers." If so, the Federal Reserve and the U.S. Treasury's close friendship with the bond dealers and brokers on Wall Street that continues to this day may become redundant. While the investment banker-Federal Reserve connection has long been hidden, hedge funds are even more reclusive because most are privately held (and thus far unregistered). If the dependence the Reserve now has on Wall Street is shifted to hedge funds, the dangers will be greater and even lesser known.

The latest move of hedge funds into the traditional business of Wall Street may be ominous. Although generally associated with short-term trading of public securities, some of the biggest hedge funds now are lenders; the loans are often for many years, adopting the role played by investment bankers. Behind their veil of secrecy, hedge funds are cutting into Wall Street's profits. Once Wall Street's best client, hedge funds have become ferocious competitors. As lenders, these funds can finance takeovers and rescues, once the exclusive province of the

corporate bond market, and most recently underwritten by commercial banks. Unlike banks, hedge funds in Greenwich and elsewhere can
conduct their secret business anywhere in the world through computer
networks without a trace.

A warning has been sounded by no less than Robert Steel, a former
vice chairman of Goldman Sachs, one of the U.S. Treasury's favorite
underwriters and a primary dealer for the Fed once snatched from
impending LTCM-related losses by Greenspan. He agrees with the
wizard about the "sophistication" of the hedge fund players. "Wall
Street is no longer where the most sophisticated capital or the most
risk appetite resides," says Steel. "Hedge funds take risk more quickly
and with more understanding than Wall Street. They are good at picking businesses where they can receive excess returns for their capital."
Further, Arthur Newman at Blackstone Group, a financial firm with
a large buyout and investment business, says that his potential customers among companies in trouble "no longer need our advice or
Wall Street's money." Moreover, the hedge funds are not above lending more than a troubled company can repay while later buying it out
as its stock falls in price.

When Krispy Kreme Doughnuts Inc. was cash starved in April
2005, both investment banks and hedge funds submitted loan proposals. The doughnut business was kept whole (though still in-the-hole)
by a $225 million refinancing from both Credit Suisse Group's Credit
Suisse First Boston and Silver Point Finance LLC, a $4 billion hedge
fund in Greenwich. The police, so fond of Krispy Kreme, have a small
hedge fund to thank for betting dollars to doughnuts.

A larger hedge fund, Cerberus, reportedly is offering financing of
buyouts. The $14 billion balance sheet of Cerberus is large for a hedge
fund, but not in the same "let's play ball" league of Wall Street investment banks or global commercial banks. Hedge funds, however, have
all that leverage that the investment banks don't have. Even if such a
fund does not approach the one hundred-to-one leveraging that undid
LTCM, Cerberus can use leverage, or borrowed cash, to give its balance sheet the $42 to $56 billion lending power that dwarfs trading
desks on Wall Street.

Hedge Funds, Treasuries and the Federal Reserve

The Wall Street-Greenspan irony is all the sweeter for this, enough to fill at least one F. Scott Fitzgerald short story: Wall Street has been lending money to these hedge funds that are cutting away at their business. In turn, the traditional business of investment banks will necessarily shrink. Eventually the Treasury may have to market its securities through hedge funds and the Federal Reserve may have to conduct open market operations through funds that have even less transparency. Then, the quiet dependence that the Reserve now has with investment and other bankers will shift to hedge funds. With so much notional (imaginary) value at stake, this is a frightening prospect.

In increasingly volatile financial markets, and with hedge funds' appetite for higher risk where the returns they chase are greater, there is no limit to their mischief. If the banks are lending to financial institutions that are buying derivatives on credit, the banks share the risks of the derivatives' holders. Alan Greenspan surely knows this; he was present when the LTCM contagion led to the Fed bailout. Perhaps Greenspan has something else in mind. Hedge funds may be the best way to end an interest-rate conundrum when it appears, as it did in summer 2005. No matter how much he talked about it, Greenspan could not talk the long-term bond rate into proper alignment above short-term rates. If the Federal Open Market Committee were trading through hedge funds, perhaps at last interest rates would converge. Truly efficient bond markets may require a mere $100 trillion in imaginary hedge fund assets.

15

GREENSPAN TAKES US
FROM GOLDILOCKS TO THE
SOFT PATCH AND
BACK AGAIN

There appears to be enough evidence, at least tentatively, to conclude that our [the Fed's] strategy of addressing the bubble's consequences rather than the bubble itself has been successful. Despite the stock market plunge, terrorist attacks, corporate scandals, and wars in Afghanistan and Iraq, we experienced an exceptionally mild recession—even milder than that of a decade earlier. ... But highly aggressive monetary ease was doubtless also a significant contributor to stability.

Alan Greenspan, "Risk and Uncertainty in Monetary Policy," remarks at the Meetings of the American Economic Association, San Diego, California, January 3, 2004.

In the collapse of the Great American Bull Market, the Internet, telecommunications and related hi-tech industries took the most punishment. It was so much the worse for Alan Greenspan's dream of the "New Economy." Just as the Jazz Age came to ruin with deflation in goods prices, so too did global deflation follow the greatest stock market collapse of the twentieth century. A fear of goods deflation, which Greenspan suddenly felt, is the most unnatural occurrence any central banker ever has. For him, it must have felt like an "out of body" personal experience. At the feet of Wall Street, Greenspan had learned only that goods inflation was evil. It, not deflation, was what he was equipped to fight. By cheering the expansion of the bubble, however, Greenspan had contributed greatly to his own worst nightmare, an enemy he has never engaged.

His misunderstanding of economic history combined with his concern with what would happen to the value of financial assets held by the wealthy led him away from backing up his "talk" with action. As the bubble was in full expansion, he supposed, however obliquely, that his role would be to take corrective action *after* the crash, thereby preventing a second Great Depression. In this light, Greenspan's ambition for the country was as modest as his personal ambition was great. First, he stood back, watching and cheering as financial asset prices soared. He even advanced a new theory about how this might be the end of history, a condition in which a "New Economy" imbued with soaring productivity had eliminated not only business cycles but stock market crashes. He had arrived at the same conclusion that he had at the feet of Ayn Rand; since The Market is perfect, mere mortals, even if they be central bankers, can make no improvements. In the end, fearing the worst, Greenspan's successful deflation of the bubble would have besmirched his legacy.

The Anatomy of Greenspan's Policies after the Bursting of the Great American Stock Market Bubble

He was wrong, on several accounts. He had to retreat into the Schumpeterian language of "creative destruction" to salvage what was left of his theory of the new global economy. He did what he had done before—post-1987 stock market crash and after the bubbles burst in East Asia, Russia and at Long-Term Capital Management. He slashed short-term interest rates. At a nominal one percent and even higher, the real fed funds rate turned negative. Ironically, John Maynard Keynes, Greenspan's nemesis, had demonstrated during the 1930s that such negative real interest rates (and more) would be required to end the Great Depression. After the bubble burst in 2000–2001, businesses were up to their eyeballs in hi-tech gear and broadband cables and were not about to make new capital investments. The stimulation of consumption was the only way out.

The Fed did what it had done only reluctantly before; it encouraged Americans to borrow more, much more. Greenspan, the financial asset prices inflator, had made demand-pull Keynesianism once again relevant. In truth, an aggressively expansive monetary and fiscal policy is the only remedy, once incompetence has allowed a deflation to take hold. Bush II did not design his tax cuts or the war in Iraq for that purpose; rather the tax policy was to protect and abet the Republican base of wealth, and the war was strangely perverse neoconservative politics. From the beginning, Greenspan knew that he had to shoulder the burden of ending this new financial and economic crisis even as he denied his contribution to it. More credit and lower interest rates were the only way out for someone who opposed with his whole being the national deficit spending at the heart of Keynes' anti-depression policy.

Since financial asset inflation was one side of a coin with stagnant working class wages the flip side, the amount of credit creation required to prevent a depression was massive. The one percent fed funds rate and record low long-term interest rates testify to that necessity. The Fed was in uncharted territory, even if it was greatly of its own creation. Americans were able to buy new autos at zero percent interest rates and new houses or their refinancing at historically low interest rates. Even credit card rates plunged for many consumers. When credit card debt got too high to service, homeowners borrowed equity from their homes, which were appreciating in price. It took a long time, but the economy recovered from a mild recession in 2001 and, over several years, new jobs were being created. Some economists began to warn that Greenspan may have replaced the stock-market bubble with a bubble in housing, which could burst.

It was time to increase the fed funds rate, however slowly, however measured. Then, we could all stand back and see what happens. Greenspan continued to worry about the financial wealth holders even as housing asset prices inflated. After all, one of the consequences of the great stock market bubble bursting was a fear of flying stock prices: uncertainty about the value of stocks and bonds would be a lasting legacy. "Stability," Greenspan's word, was a strange choice to describe the aftermath of the great financial asset destruction of 2000–2001, no matter how creative.

A Brief Goldilocks Interlude

Some years later, by the time the American Economic Association had convened its annual meeting for 2004, considerable calm *had* been restored. The financial market players once again enjoyed a Goldilocks Economy generally between summer and the end of 2004. To the great discomfort of Wall Street, however, more than three bears seemed to be coming out of hibernation by the end of the first quarter of 2005. Things were not looking so hot, certainly not warm. The Dow Jones Industrial Average slipped 128.43 points, or one point two six percent, to 10070.37 on Thursday, April 28. Blue chips were down four point one percent for April and six point six percent for the first quarter of 2005. A reported first-quarter slowing of *estimated* GDP to three point one percent—falling short of an expected three point five percent yearly—was one small fly in the soup. Worse, the horse fly in the soup

OLIPHANT © (2000) UNIVERSAL PRESS SYNDICATE. Reprinted with permission. All rights reserved.

was an increase in the inflation index *most watched by Alan Greenspan.* The GDP report, which understated an unexpected improvement in the international trade balance, was preliminary, but it didn't seem to matter. Greenspan already had told the market early in the year that the economy was in a "soft patch."

The financial wealth holders were buying bonds because they believed, wrongly, that Greenspan would pause in his thus far steadfast march toward higher and higher short-term interest rates. As ever, those who had bought stocks after summer 2005 did so in a belief that moderate economic growth and modest or no inflation would support the market through the year. Inflation, so they believe, cuts into profits because it gets fed into rising wages and unit production costs. To square the circle, Greenspan has raised interest rates when inflation has been a distant figment of his imagination, raising borrowing costs of home buyers and small business firms, further eroding profits and inviting a business recession.

Memories of Stagflation

Back in the 1970s and early 1980s, the combination of slow growth and rising inflation earned and deserved the name, stagflation. This dynamic duo was mostly the result of the success in OPEC's tripling crude oil prices. Stagflation is considered a poor environment for stocks because the "stag" reduces sales and profits while the "flation" scares eventually send interest rates higher. Rather than stagflation, the new situation seemed closer—mixing a metaphor—to a Mexican standoff. In 2005, more modest oil price increases in a more oil-efficient economy were adding more to the stagnation than to the inflation. If nonetheless the stagnation is more worrisome than the new but still modest inflation, large investment institutions and eventually small buyers will sell some of their stock holdings and buy more bonds. If Greenspan stops raising rates in a weakening economy, bonds could outperform stocks. While some shareholders believed the slowdown to be temporary, they nonetheless were nervous—not just about a slowing global economy but with the prospects for further fed funds rate hikes and even higher oil prices.

This may sound familiar because it is. Even as he has promoted "transparency" in markets, Greenspan has been creating confusion. If we understand confusion as a source of uncertainty, we can slice through the Greenspanspeak fog. More often than not, Greenspan has expressed more uncertainty than he feels; he apparently is fairly sure about the probabilities of a, b or c happening. The financial market players, who watch Greenspan before they even glance at the markets, are nervous because they don't know what to do in an uncertain environment. Uncertainty is never the friend of financial wealth holders. This nervousness has reached clinical levels since the Nasdaq crash; despite his sincere efforts, the Fed chairman has not helped matters.

It has been a venerable Greenspan pattern. Whenever a new kind of business condition develops—more often than not caused by Fed policies—Alan Greenspan has invented a new word for it. Worse, he latter either denies using the term or says that he regrets the whole thing. The economy, Greenspan now tells us, is in a "soft patch." This would not be so scary if he had not used the term earlier to describe an earlier dismal summer. Even scarier is that no one knows for sure what Greenspan means by "soft patch," leaving us with no guide to when a once "soft" place becomes a hard patch.

Somewhere Between a Soft Patch and the Briar Patch

Synonyms for "soft" include squishy, spongy, elastic, limp, and pliable. Synonyms for "patch" include scrap, area, insignia, piece, and bit. Take your pick. Does the wizard mean that the economy is in a squishy insignia, pliable scrap, elastic area, limp piece, or spongy bit? Whatever, it must be the *flip side* of a hard patch. The synonyms for "hard" are potentially more intriguing, and they include firm, stiff, rigid, and tough. So, the economy could be in a place *the opposite of* a rigid insignia, hard bit, firm scrap, or tough piece. Clearly, we suppose, a "hard patch," a place Greenspan is unwilling to go, is easier to understand and even to identify. Other permutations (along with still more synonyms and antonyms) I leave to the imaginations of others.

A hard patch would take us into a different fable and a new character. It was Peter Rabbit who found himself in a briar patch. What we have perhaps is the collision of two fables, leaving all of us between a soft patch and a hard place. During much of 2004, Baby Bear was eating soup that Wall Street considered neither too hot or too cold, but just right. On her way home, Goldilocks might have found herself in a briar patch by the first quarter of 2005 with a tough piece to go.

The soft patch on the way to a hard place may turn out to have been an unnecessary detour led by rising interest rates in a soft economy. The American economy had been on the verge of a depression before the Federal Reserve had lowered the Fed funds rate target to near zero (below zero adjusted for goods inflation). During those same years, the George W. administration was greatly expanding federal deficits through war financing and lowering tax rates for rich folks. It took this combination of monetary and accidental fiscal expansion to prevent the U.S. economy from slipping beneath the waves of global expansion elsewhere. Alan Greenspan now had simply diverted Goldilocks from the path normally taken and down a primrose lane to a harder place.

Goldilocks in Springtime

By late May 2005, optimism about an expanding economy without inflation was taking hold. Sentiment had shifted back to the Goldilocks fable which explained why the wealth holders saw the need to buy more stocks on any and all the frequent dips in stock prices. The initially revised estimate for first quarter GDP was a nice round three point five percent, not fast enough to add new jobs to the labor market, not slow enough to signal a recession and the need to lower interest rates until the economy was growing "too fast" again. Greenspan had temporarily, though unintentionally, hurt some equity and bond holders. Traders came out of what was thought to be a briar patch in droves; now they were betting that the release of the minutes from the latest Federal Open Market Committee (FOMC) meeting on May 2 and other information, would further feed a non-inflationary expansion theme so dear to the storytellers on Wall Street, one that would continue to keep the job market soft. The Goldilocks Economy was back, but for how long, and at what cost to ordinary American wage earners?

The answer came quickly. The third time the first quarter GDP was estimated, it was five point eight percent, sufficiently high to create new jobs. "Too many jobs" has never been a good thing for the maestro. In late June, Greenspan and the FOMC raised the fed funds rate target another quarter point to three point two five percent and announced that the "measured" increases would continue. It was the ninth consecutive quarter-point increase. Surely something more was behind the most recent fed funds rate increases. Interest rate hikes cannot lower the price of crude oil except through the creation of unemployment and still lower wages. The unemployed then can't afford gas at the pump but luckily have nowhere to go; they can park their cars at home. The FOMC stated that "pressures on inflation remain elevated," though growth had "slowed somewhat." But, except for oil, where was the inflation? Well, there was inflation in one thing, and it was not a good but an asset, housing.

Truth and Consequences

No matter how vigorously denied by the wizard, the stock market bubble ending the 1990s was principally a Greenspan creation. Once he had decided to live with the Great Bull Market in stocks, the stock market bubble and its aftermath was assured. Bubbles always burst. It would be magnificent if they could simply float away, but they don't. The next set of problems involve coping with Greenspan's remedy. The Fed had created another asset bubble.

16

THE HOUSING
BUBBLE CONUMDRUM

*American consumers might benefit if lenders provided greater mortgage
product alternatives to the traditional fixed-rate mortgage.
The traditional fixed-rate mortgage may be an
expensive method of financing a home.*

Alan Greenspan advocating the use of adjustable rate mortgages in a
speech to the Credit Union National Association, 2004.

*[Home equity loans] are subject to increased risk if
interest rates rise and home values decline.*

Part of a warning from the Fed and other bank regulators
about loans related to housing with adjustable rates
issued in mid-May, 2005.

Alan Greenspan never thought that his days of dealing with bubbles
had ended with the 1987 stock market crash and the total unraveling
of the Nasdaq in 2000–2001. By now he was claiming "risk management" to be the main role for the Federal Reserve. Greenspan and his
neoconservative cousins had created enough risks to make risk management a growth industry. Again, Mr. Greenspan and company were
busily creating conditions so volatile that only a whirling dervish could
dodge them all.

Thanks to the stock market bubble and especially the bursting of
Nasdaq, wealthy people and institutions needed to shift their funds into
different assets. Those thirty-five to fifty percent returns in securities
had essentially disappeared except in hedge funds which were again
under pressure, some even collapsing. The housing market, especially

second homes, vacation homes and investment condos became the new playground for the rich. Ultimately, as ever, families that couldn't afford to play did get in on the action and would be the most vulnerable, just as they are in stock market crashes. There have little to lose, but it is all they have.

How the Fed Can Stimulate Housing Construction and Demand

The conventional wisdom among real-estate, finance and economics professors is that a bubble cannot form in housing—in part, because housing is not simply straw, brick or timber, but Home Sweet Home. Reminding ourselves that the current conventional wisdom is the equivalent of conservative ideology and Greenspan is an ideologue, we naturally expect him to take the same position. We need recall, however in the interest of full Fed disclosure, Greenspan's pattern of taking opposing stances on everything, sometimes on the same day, in the same speech.

Though usually never mentioned, the housing and construction industries are central to Fed policy. At some risk of repetition, we review the effects of the Fed's open market operations. To stimulate business activity, the Fed provides more reserves to banks for overnight lending (as fed funds). In turn, this act of increasing the reserves in the banking system lowers short-term interest rates. Since private banks "mark-up" all other loans such as the prime rate from the fed funds rate, the interest rates of longer maturities are lowered. The first effects are to reduce interest rates on credit cards issued by these private banks. Next, housing and construction are especially stimulated by lower interest rates. Employment and incomes in those industries increase, thus stimulating other parts of the economy. To slow down business activity, the Fed provides fewer funds to banks for overnight lending so as to hopefully raise interest rates across the spectrum. In turn, credit card debt is reduced and the construction industry slows down, eventually taking most of the balance of the economy with it. In these two processes, overall credit is expanded and contracted.

Asset Inflation in Housing

The first signs that the beneficial side of rising home values were vanishing emerged near the end of 2003. Prior to the death of irrational exuberance, the foundation of rapidly growing wealth was in securities. The equity ascent—off to a flying start after 1994, peaking in early 2000, reaching its apogee in 2002—was a source of great accumulations of wealth at the very top. Wealthy bond holders also did remarkably well. Those ordinary people with financial assets in their pension plans went along for the ride, but also for the fall. The value of real estate, which is somewhat more democratically held, lagged, but began to accelerate well before the bottoming of equity prices, becoming horrifyingly evident in 2004.

For an interminable time, Alan Greenspan denied that the U.S. was in the early stages or *any* stages of a housing bubble. He noted the great demand among hardworking immigrants for houses (on Greg Norman's exclusive golf course resorts?). Housing, he said too, is a local market, making it virtually impossible to experience a national housing bubble. Moreover, he added, it's hard to speculate in a house a family lives in because, when they sell, they have to buy another and pay all those closing costs.

Despite Greenspan's romantic window on poor immigrants, a realist should not be surprised to find that rich people own more mansions and estates than the poor or the middle class. Although it may be embarrassing to the neoconservative wealthy family to see typical families benefit from asset inflation, the transfer of wealth out of securities and into large homes, as well as into palatial second homes on beaches and golf courses, did not leave *upper* middle class households behind. Aided by exotic financing innovations so praised by Greenspan, many were buying homes and condos that they couldn't afford.

At a time when an article in the *Wall Street Journal* by James R. Hagerty was raising a few red flags, Greenspan continued to say that there was no bubble in housing. However, the oracle's past record in bubble spotting ranks right up there with the captain of the *Titanic* in spotting serious icebergs. Greenspan once said that there is no way to identify a bubble until it bursts; he also told fellow economists on January 3, 2004: "...our strategy of addressing the bubble's [the Nasdaq bubble] consequences rather than the bubble itself has been successful." Although the economists at the AEA gave him a standing ovation and muttered about his greatness, others were reminded of the inadequacy of the life boats on the *Titanic*. If the captain of money policy chose not to address a "bubble" that he could not identify but nonetheless dealt with "its" consequences, doesn't this mean that he knew of a bubble before and after?

Spotting a Housing Bubble

As with the Nasdaq, it *is* possible to know a bubble when it pops up. A bubble in housing prices is different but has some shared characteristics. Buying is based only on anticipation of rising prices rather than on fundamentals. Expectations of returns are based on recent gains rather than on historic norms. Some historical norms can change, but not over a fortnight. Buyers lose all respect for risk and refuse to believe that higher returns are closely linked to higher risks. In housing, as in other assets, at some price the focal perceived risk is "not being on board" rather than "possibly losing money." Minds lose the battle of rationality against irrationality to greed.

Greed and agreed, housing is different in an important respect: We can't inhabit the shares of Microsoft stock, no matter how many shares we have. Normally, buying and selling properties requires paying commissions and other "transactions costs." Normally, it takes months or even a year to sell a house above the current market price. As finance people put it, the market for houses is not as liquid as that for securities; it takes considerable time to "cash out" of a house or other property.

Nonetheless, a house is a home only in normal times. It is precisely when a house isn't a home that a housing bubble exists. During a bubble, price appreciation overwhelms six percent commissions and closing costs; besides there are ways to buy at pre-construction costs that require no costs before the deal is closed and the property can be resold (flipped) before closing time. During a bubble, a house can be sold the day it goes on the market. What normally is an illiquid market becomes liquid. Besides, through a process called securitization, a bundle of real estate properties can be packaged and resold as a piece of paper; houses are converted not to homes, but to derivatives.

Still, Greenspan has a point about real estate markets being local. Real estate agents live and die on that premise. Of course, this idea is modified by securitization or even by real estate management trusts (REITS). All of which brings us back to the *Wall Street Journal.*

James Hagerty cites a study by house-price gurus Karl E. Case of Wellesley College and Robert J. Shiller of Yale University; they find that national measures of housing trends can be misleading. While house prices rise gradually along with the slow growth in most families' personal incomes, states with cities short of land for residential construction such as in California (Bakersfield, Riverside-San Bernardino, Los Angeles-Long Beach, Redding, Fresno, San Diego, Orange County) and coastal Florida (West Palm Beach-Boca Raton, Miami, Fort Myers-Cape Coral, Fort Lauderdale) are more likely to swing from boom to bust in a hurry. The Case-Shiller view would seem, at first *rougissent*, to support the view of Coe Lewis, an agent at Century 21 Award who says that people worry too much about prices. "They get paralyzed," Ms. Lewis says. "They almost overthink the process. They think there's got to be a dip. There's not going to be a dip. I'm not afraid at all of a bubble in Southern California."

Greenspan Gets Smarter as the Bubble Gets Bigger

With the Wall *Street Journal* ahead of the pack, by early spring 2005 business analysts in the United States seemingly could not write or speak of anything other than a herd instinct in the housing market itself. Case and Shiller began to refer to a national bubble. Alan Greenspan, so early to cry wolf about Dow stock prices, joined this hunt very late in the season. At last, in response to questions following a luncheon speech on May 20, 2005, he told the Economic Club of New York: "At a minimum, there's a little froth in the market. We don't perceive that there is a national bubble, but it's hard not to see that there are a lot of local bubbles." In frothing about "local" bubbles, Greenspan appears to endorse the earlier Case-Shiller view. Besides "lather" and "fizz," however, a synonym for froth is "bubbles." The man who once claimed that bubbles cannot be found until they burst now finds bubbles all over the place, including locally. "Local" can mean "narrow" so he may be speaking of only tiny bubbles.

While Greenspan is notorious for saying one thing and meaning another or claiming one thing but denying he meant what they say he said, he generally has recognized a financial disaster after it has happened. We have to worry then when we see the maestro going so quickly from "it can't happen" to "froth" which means bubbles. As to what is local, in the Case-Shiller study, there are so many local-bubbles cities in California to make it a bubble state. California's economy is about the size of the United Kingdom's. If California and Florida were merged into the "Sunshine Boys," their economy would about equal Germany's. In a country where Treasury officials worry about how a U.K. or Germany business recession might adversely affect Americans, California and Florida are essentially countries within the U.S. As to Century 21 Award, it is a national franchise, so frothy local speeches by its agents are suspect.

As to a housing bubble, "Greenspan" is likely to be correct, but *which* Greenspan? His inability to recognize (or at least admit to) the greatest financial bubble in world history is not encouraging. The Federal Reserve, the organization he happened to be heading at the time, issued some modest new guidelines to mortgage lenders during the same week as Greenspan's "frothy" speech. Among regulators top concerns is the surge in popularity of interest-only loans, which allow people to pay only interest in the initial years but face the entire principal later. If there really is a bubble, however, toothlessly mouthed warnings will not stop most lenders from lending as usual. Was, in fact, Greenspan again saying one thing and doing another? He and other Fed officials denied that they were continuing to raise interest rates to slow housing asset inflation.

Once enough people believe that a bubble will continue to expand, it probably will. Once four-fifths of *Wall Street Journal* readers believe (as reported May 2005) that there is a housing bubble, it is a short step from believing that a bubble will continue and believing that not participating in it will be a lost opportunity. *Wall Street Journal* subscribers have the wealth to keep it going in California and Florida. The August 12, 2005 *Journal*'s "House of the Week" was a 106-room, 11-bedroom, 13-bathroom little fix-me-up mansion for $21.5 million and it was in the Berkshires of Massachusetts, not even in California. When sky-high prices are accepted as "normal," much as Greenspan ultimately decided that Internet and tech stock prices were just what the market ordered during the late 1990s, look out below!

Greenspan's Innocent Hypocrisy in His Attack on Fannie and Freddie

Fannie Mae and Freddie Mac were both chartered by the U.S. Congress to help finance housing for the typical family. They buy residential mortgage loans from lenders and bundle the loans into securities. Since these securities can be traded, mortgage market liquidity has been increased and interest costs lowered (enhanced "market efficiency," in Greenspanspeak). As government-sponsored enterprises (GSEs), Fannie and Freddie fall under some affordable housing goals.

These mortgage purchase quotas require that no less than half of the mortgages they purchase be for low- and moderate-income households, that a fifth be set aside for those of low income, and that slightly less than a third be from geographically targeted underserved areas. In a housing bubble, finding an affordable house becomes difficult, especially as mortgage interest rates rise.

Fannie and Freddie now use derivatives in interest-rate swaps, just like commercial banks. In a typical swap, a borrower with a variable-rate loan and a borrower with a fixed-rate loan "swap" their interest-payment obligations to better match debt to assets. Fannie and Freddie use such swaps because as interest rates change, so does the likelihood that the mortgages they hold will be paid off early, before maturity. Moreover, like banks and other corporations, they issue equity so that stock can be bought and sold in these GSEs.

Alan Greenspan not only is a long-time critic of Fannie and Freddie, recently he has—with ample backing from the Treasury and White House—urged Congress to put severe limits on their business. The irony here blends nicely with hypocrisy. The Congress created the GSEs as *private* business enterprises. Moreover, while the Fed buys short-term securities from commercial banks to set short-term interest rates, Fannie and Freddie buy mortgages from the banks to bundle for resale and keep long-term rates lower. Except for particular goals set by the U.S. Congress, both the Fed and the GSEs are *independent*. Perhaps it is sibling rivalry: in many ways the Fed and the GSEs are similar creatures.

Their differences, however, disturb Mr. Greenspan, as the czar of all financial markets. The Fed is cozy with banks; Fannie and Freddie compete with the mortgage business of banks. Alan Greenspan's main self-appointed task is to serve Wall Street and the wealth holders; Fannie and Freddie's main responsibility is to insure affordable housing for low- and moderate-income families. Worse, in Greenspan's view, the GSEs are "subsidized" by the "perception" that they are "too big to fail" and would be bailed out by the government. He also is concerned about Fannie and Freddie's lack of sophistication in handling derivatives. Worst of all, Fannie and Freddie are not fully subject to "market discipline."

As Greenspan has put it, "the existence, or even the perception, of government backing undermines the effectiveness of market discipline." This "special relationship to the government" is the root evil. Greenspan not only wants the GSEs regulated on par with banks but also have the size of their mortgage portfolio limited. While there are some legitimate concerns with the operations of Fannie and Freddie, they should not be stones on which Greenspan grinds his free-market fundamentalist axe to serve Wall Street interests.

His hypocrisy may be innocent, but it nonetheless triumphs. Mr. Greenspan helped to create banks such as Citigroup, now too big to fail. Doubtless Citigroup will be bailed out by the Fed, because, as the *smaller* Citicorp, it already has been—*twice*—indirectly, along with others, in the Long-Term Capital Management bailout, and on its own mismanagement. Citigroup apparently is sufficiently sophisticated to use derivatives (though it failed to use them properly); Fannie and Freddie can't be trusted with swaps (though they have used them properly). With only ten banks controlling half of all domestic banking assets in the United States, why the great concern with the holdings of Fannie and Freddie at a time when their share of the mortgage market is declining? The sincere problem seems to be this: Fannie and Freddie make it slightly more difficult for Wall Street and other financial institutions to transfer wealth to the top. Under the Greenspan Standard, Fannie and Freddie's loans are "non-conforming."

Summing-up

Meanwhile, will the housing bubble burst? The most critical consideration is the ability of speculators to make monthly payments. This ability depends on two things: income and mortgage rates. According to Federal Reserve data, the debt-to-income ratio of U.S. households reached a "Rocky Mountain high" in the fourth quarter of 2004 of one point two-to-one at very low mortgage rates. A decade earlier it had been zero point nine-to-one. Moreover, household debt as a share of household assets also is nearing an all-time high even as the value of household assets is being inflated by rising home prices. Though it isn't the kind of leveraging known to hedge funds, households nonetheless are taking on more risk. A crisis such as the international financial crises of 1997–1998 could send interest-rates soaring for those holding mortgages with adjustable rates and speed bankruptcies.

Now, irony grasps us and will not let go. Alan Greenspan has been the major cheerleader for the current housing boom, as he was with the dot-com and tech stocks. His good cheer has been slightly muffled by the Fed's increasing short-term interest rates at a "measured pace," while encouraging the bond market players—influential in deciding mortgage rates—to do the same. That mortgage rates declined during 12 months ending June 2005 while the Fed funds rate target was being increased eight times was Greenspan's "conundrum," requiring that the fed funds rate climb continue unabated—to keep inflationary expectations in check, he claims. In the August 2005 FOMC meeting, however, housing prices dominated the discussion.

The strengthening rebound in the Dow combined with soaring house prices could produce the kind of double bubble that undid the Japanese financial system and economy in the early 1990s. Despite the creation by HedgeStreet of a "hedgelet" that allows individual investors to speculate on the direction of home values in major cities, it is unlikely that new derivatives will bring stability to financial or to housing markets any time soon. Besides, like the financial bubble that led to an aftermath that led to the Fed's low interest-rate policy, the fortunes of the economy have shifted mostly to one industry. Employment in housing and housing-related industries accounted for about forty-three percent of the rise in private-sector payrolls between late 2001 and mid-2005, while the industry accounted for about two percentage points of the annualized GDP growth rate during 2004–2005. Without the housing boom, the GDP growth rate would have been about one point five percent and the official unemployment rate somewhere around twelve percent. Much of Greenspan's final legacy depends on the Fed's ability to bring high-flying houses in for a soft landing, even as he denies that the Fed is targeting housing.

17

SOCIAL SECURITY: ON THE CUTTING EDGE OF FEDERAL BUDGET DEFICITS

Alan Greenspan said a week ago that faster payroll tax increases and reduced cost-of-living adjustments for beneficiaries are needed.

New York Times columnist Deborah Rankin reporting on Greenspan's views as chairman of President Reagan's commission on Social Security, 1983. His proposed tax increases and reduced benefits were adopted by the U.S. Congress.

The current Social Security system is "not working;" private accounts "which I approve of" would "not alleviate the current problem," which would "require tax increases and benefit reductions."

From Alan Greenspan's testimony and responses to questions about President George W. Bush's proposed "reform" of Social Security before the U.S. Senate Banking Committee, February 17, 2005.

When we think of Social Security or fiscal policy, Alan Greenspan is not the first name that comes to mind, even if we are thinking of his retirement. The federal budgetary process amends government expenditures as well as tax rates, which in turn influence government revenues. Fiscal policy is intentionally changing taxes or expenditures to stabilize the economy. Although these funds flow in and out of the U.S. Treasury, the U.S. Congress writes the fiscal year budgets, often working from budget bills written at the White House. During the George W. Bush Administration the White House generally has had its way with budgets since Republican majorities control both houses of Congress.

"Having its way" hit a roadblock with an ill-fated plan to "overhaul" Social Security in the year 2005.

The Social Security system, established as part of Franklin Roosevelt's New Deal program in 1935, is a payroll tax-financed Trust Fund independent of the general revenues of government. It was a pay-as-you-retire system in which the Trust Fund was collecting in revenue roughly what it was paying out. The Federal Reserve has *no* legislated role to play in decisions related to fiscal policy, much less Social Security. Alan Greenspan nonetheless has repeatedly influenced tax and budget policies, as well as being a powerful voice contributing to the death of fiscal policy. And he began effectively meddling in America's most important social program for the elderly way back in 1983 and continues to do so.

There may be as much consistency as irony in Greenspan and, most likely, successor Fed chair's insistence that no president and no legislature get in the way of the Fed. Since his Fed's independence is a one-way street, Greenspan decided early—even before his appointment to the Reserve—that *he* should decide the course of fiscal policy, not the president, not the Congress. His reasons why the Congress and the president should keep their "hands off" government taxation and spending are the same as for why they should keep "hands off" the Reserve. Since neither the Congress nor the President of the United States has the maturity and the discipline to keep a lid on the Federal budget, either's control of the money supply would leave the world in ruins. In turn, Greenspan's outlook on Social Security "reform"—long and strongly-held views—is deeply influenced by his take on federal deficits.

Greenspan Meddles in Fiscal Affairs

Alan Greenspan, riding Reagan's coattails on the way to Greenspanmailing Bill Clinton, defined the rhetoric of government taxation and expenditure. Greenspanspeak has diverted public attention away from a quarter century of stagnant wages and job insecurity and toward the *dire consequences* of federal budget deficits and the advantages of surpluses. In this there is enough hypocrisy to swathe both the Reserve and the White House. Alan Greenspan and Wall Street tell us—and, never mind that the evidence mounts against it—that federal deficits cause inflation in all instances except one—when the federal deficits are caused by tax cuts for the very rich. Thus, federal deficits are bad news because goods inflation truly *is* bad news for the exclusive membership of the wealth holding class. There nonetheless remains the residue of Greenspan and Wall Street's hidden agenda: they want to reduce the size of government, whether it is by diminishing its revenues from the rich or from restricting its spending on poor and middle class families.

Greenspan played a cat and mouse game with President George W. Bush, who never met a tax cut for the rich that he didn't like. When George, the W, was appointed President by the U.S. Supreme Court in 2000, he saw it as a mandate to reduce the taxes of America's richest families. Greenspan has counseled presidents from Ford to Clinton against cutting taxes *before* balancing the budget by first cutting spending. He even opposed expenditure increases after the federal budget swung to a surplus in 1998 for the first time in 30 years. At first, Greenspan was reluctant to support W's tax cuts because he was not sure that forecasted budget surpluses would be sufficient to provide a dividend for the rich without creating a deficit. The maestro's conversion came at a providential time and was of biblical proportions. After all, Mr. Bush had been sworn in (his hand on a family Bible) days earlier on a platform of tax cuts.

In January 2001, the president had the unqualified support of Alan Greenspan. The Chairman was telling the Senate that "the most recent data significantly raise the probability that sufficient resources will be available to undertake both debt reduction" *and* tax cuts. Democrats were appalled (*why* has escaped explanation). Greenspan knew perfectly well how much weight his public imprimatur carries. The maestro's performance was déjà vu all over again; he had helped Reagan secure tax cuts for the rich and payroll tax increases on workers through Social Security "reform." As a hedge, something Greenspan understood from derivatives, he suggested that the Bush tax cuts be automatically canceled if debt targets are missed. Needless to say, all those who depended upon elections for their jobs rejected this advice.

Tax Cuts for the Rich Have Unintended Consequences

It is one thing to be blind-sighted, but quite another to be blind-sighted by one's own blindness. Greenspan had waxed poetically about how the "New Economy" had been forged out of historically high productivity improvements. Productivity accelerated but the most significant contributor to tax revenue growth was the late 1990s stock bubble that Greenspan greatly contributed to. The bubble generated a tidal wave of tax revenue from stock-trading profits, corporate CEO bonuses, and withdrawals from retirement plans. Tax revenue had fluctuated between seventeen and nineteen percent of gross domestic product for a half century. Suddenly, in the year 2000, it surged—like Noah's flood—to twenty-one percent. Dr. Greenspan seemingly failed to consider how much of that would go south *when*, not *if*, the stock bubble burst.

Anyway, to cut a long story short, tax revenue fell short of projections by May 2001. By 2004, after that business recession and three grand rounds of tax cuts, tax revenue fell to a forty-five low of sixteen percent of GDP. Gigantic federal budget surpluses had been converted, like a prince into a frog, into gigantic federal budget deficits. Amazingly, early in 2003 the White House pressed for a fourth round of tax cuts.

The persistence of irony is sufficient to make us suspect alchemy, if not other bad puns. Much earlier, Dr. Greenspan had convinced W.'s father to urge the passage of a bill requiring tax cuts be offset with spending cuts. This idea was close to Greenspan's heart because it would assure the contraction of the size of the government. Alas, Papa Bush's bill expired in 2002. Some argued for restoration of the rule, noting the support of "no less an observer than Alan Greenspan." But, the traditional country club Republicans replied: "We don't believe that you should have to 'pay for' tax cuts." And, so, Hamlet-like, Republicans defeated the effort on a party-line vote; like the son, they had revolted against the father.

We next turn to the strangely connected dalliance of Alan Greenspan with Social Security "reform."

TOLES © (2005) The Washington Post. Reprinted with permission of UNIVERSAL PRESS SYNDICATE. All right reserved.

Greenspan and Retirement Benefits—His and Ours

Every year, about the time that summer becomes insufferably hot and muggy in Washington, D.C. and in Kansas City, the Federal Reserve Bank of Kansas City hosts a conference in lovely and cool Jackson Hole, Wyoming. The setting is perfect. At the end of the valley rests one of the Rockefeller estates while the Grand Teton Mountains, named as only the French would, stand full-breasted over the gathering. Carefully selected academics attend the conferences to stimulate discussions quickly forgotten. It rather is a *simulated* tit-for-tat or, the French might say, *vice versa*, that serves the higher purpose of simulated democracy at the American central bank.

As full disclosure, I must admit having been to both a Rockefeller estate (in New York) *and* to Jackson Hole. My first visit to Jackson Hole was afoot, making it all the more memorable. I was seventeen years of age, unemployed in Mt. Morris, Ill., but seeking employment in distant California. My friend, "Red," and I were hitchhiking to the land of golden opportunity. On the way, we were picked up (appropriately, in a pick-up truck) by Bob Lotta, a rancher who had once been a liberal candidate for governor of the great but essentially vacant state of Wyoming. He didn't win, but a liberal democrat eventually did become governor. Lotta—of French heritage, of course—hired Red and me as "ranch-hands" at his (now) dude ranch on Lava Creek, just east of the mountain range overlooking Jackson Hole, while another Rockefeller estate rests at the end of the valley.

At age seventeen, retirement certainly was not on my mind, but it has since intruded, as it has for Alan Greenspan. Bob Lotta had no retirement plan, though his ranching business already had gone the way of tourism on the way to the Fed meetings at Jackson Hole. In contrast, Alan Greenspan has long had retirement programs, several for himself and another for ordinary Americans. The Federal Reserve System has one of the best retirement systems in the world. Besides, Greenspan, the libertarian, has spent most of his working career as a federal government employee; he thus enjoys multiple retirement programs. And, besides that, he has substantial private wealth. And, besides even that, he married NBC News correspondent Andrea Mitchell. Before marrying they dated for twelve years.

Until April 1997 and his marriage to Andrea, Greenspan had most of his personal assets in a blind trust. He then liquidated that trust so the couple could make joint financial plans; presumably their finances remained laissez faire during their dating years. At the end of 1997, his $3.5 million in financial assets were mostly in short-term Treasury bills ($2.4 million) and in bonds ($600,000). He held mostly T-bills, he said, "to avoid any conflict of interest." Since the Fed conducts monetary policy by buying and selling T-bills, this is like the head of the Securities and Exchange Commission saying that he holds only stocks "to avoid any conflict of interest."

New disclosure forms only require Greenspan to provide figures in broad ranges. In 2004 his assets were valued between $3.3 million and $6.4 million, about the same as in 2003. His holdings are in money-market accounts and U.S. Treasury securities. Greenspan's wife, Andrea, had separate financial holdings valued between about $1 million and $2.5 million in 2004. Although Greenspan "avoids any appearance of conflict that might be raised by stock holdings in individual companies," Mitchell's holdings include stock in Abbott Laboratories, Anheuser Busch Companies, H.J. Heinz, Wal-Mart, Kimberly Clark and Pfizer. Apparently they never discuss her stock holdings even though Greenspan had liquidated his blind trust so that he and Andreas could make joint decisions.

Greenspan Chairs Reagan's Presidential Commission and "Reforms" Social Security

Greenspan was not born yesterday. He has long been staying awake at night worrying about how to cut the benefits programs for the elderly. Way back in 1983 he helped Ronald Reagan "save" Social Security.

Although Greenspan had little confidence in Ronald Reagan's economic intelligence, they shared a free-market ideology. As an economic advisor to Reagan, Greenspan probably was the most influential "outside" force behind the Reagan Administration's tax cut proposals for the richest Americans in 1981. In December of that year, Reagan appointed Alan Greenspan as chair of a presidential commission to "save" Social Security. The greatest danger to Social Security turned out to be from Mr. Greenspan and from Mr. Reagan.

While it is true that the Social Security Trust Fund "faced" a deficit, even conservative estimates put the shortfall 30 to 75 years down the fiscal road or when the baby boomers would be retiring. Reagan and Greenspan nonetheless declared that the crisis was *now*. Any time that Greenspan has chaired a committee, it usually gets his way. Greenspan wanted taxes raised on workers' wages and their benefits reduced. So, in a major overhaul of the Social Security System, Greenspan's taxing ideas were passed as Social Security Amendments in April 1983. Cost-of-living benefit increases were postponed for six months (indexed yearly rather than twice yearly), the employee payroll tax was raised, and the self-employment tax was jacked up dramatically. It forced new federal employees to join the system, increased the retirement age gradually from 65 to 67 by 2027, and applied federal income taxes on the benefits of higher-wage retirees. The 1983 law also reconfirmed a

long-established principle that the Trust Fund proceeds would be sep-
arated from the government's general revenue (from income taxes).
The Trust Fund then would have a *surplus* going out to the year 2056.

What happened next raises Mr. Greenspan's hypocrisy to, as he
might put it, "an unsustainable level." Once the new, higher Social
Security tax became effective, the surplus revenue in the Trust Fund
was used mostly, if not entirely, to pay for the massive shortfall in general
federal revenues. As before, the Trust Fund surplus was used to make
the federal budget deficits smaller and thus more politically correct.
Those general budget shortfalls were the result of the massive tax cuts
for the rich that Greenspan had helped design for Mr. Reagan! The
effect of these tax cuts assured that the Social Security surpluses would
be misused; indeed, off-setting the budget deficit was the only way that
Congress could avoid rescinding the massive tax cuts for the rich.

A long-time critic of Social Security and the New Deal, Greenspan
was finally in a position to do it the damage he thought it deserved.
After assuring a tax cut for the rich, the maestro had conducted an
assault on working Americans.

Greenspan and George W. Demand Still More Benefit Cuts and Tax Increases for Social Security c. 2005

What, we might ask, is Greenspan's current retirement plan for other
Americans? It is rare that a "public" official has an opportunity to leverage their damage two-fold. What happened more recently would nearly
equal Howard Roark's blowing up his housing project for the poor
twice. After assuring the passage of still another tax cut for the rich—
this one for George W. Bush, Greenspan puts both shoulders behind
the president's plan to *again* raise payroll taxes and reduce Social Security benefits. Worse, he gave the president desperately needed support
for privatizing part of the program.

As Greenspan put it, the aging American population, he apparently
included, face difficult choices. Greenspan, then 78 years of age (and
expected to retire in 2006 just short of age 80), made the difficult
choice of continuing as Fed chair at a modest salary of about $175,000
but with full retirement benefits, more millions of dollars in Treasuries
by now, and Andrea Mitchell. The retirement age for receiving full

Social Security benefits, already scheduled to rise from sixty-five to sixty-seven (thanks to Mr. Greenspan's 1983 "reform" effort), should be further increased. He also proposed further trimming the annual cost-of-living adjustment retirees receive by indexing benefits to the current Consumer Price Index (CPI) and away from the current wages index that has been growing at about twice the CPI rate. In this way, cost-of-living increments would be slashed in half.

Beginning in February 2004, Greenspan delivered a series of warnings about the looming crisis in Social Security and, more important, Medicare, before the first wave of 77 million U.S. baby boomers begins retiring later in the decade. He told Congress that the current Social Security system is "not working." Not working for whom? This is an insurance program that has prevented the poverty rate for those over sixty-five from soaring to forty percent (fifty-three percent for women). The truly huge problem, in Greenspan's view, is what Social Security and Medicare payments will do to soaring *federal budget deficits.* While this is convenient rhetoric borrowed directly without attribution from the financial wealth holders on Wall Street, the Social Security system was established as a separate self-funding agency, independent of the federal budget. Greenspan knows this because the Federal Reserve is similarly established. Besides, it already was *his* idea that Social Security surpluses *not* be used to offset budget deficits (caused by the huge tax cuts for the rich that he successfully supported).

There he goes again! Greenspan is pleading to save the Social Security system that he had already "rescued." Worse, he wants to apply the same remedy as before, with the addition of private accounts that would put more money in Wall Street's pockets but less in workers, eventually destroying the system. Luckily, as of this writing, American common sense has prevailed and a majority of Americans opposing the Greenspan-Bush Social Security "reform" plan has forced a Republican Congress to reject it (at least, for now). In this process, Greenspan has been more honest than George W. Bush. The Pope of Wall Street has never said that this country should have a Social Security system as a way of avoiding poverty for retired workers in their aging years. No; he consistently has attempted to minimize the overall size of government while government provides enhanced benefits to the wealth holders.

18

GETTING PERSONAL
WITH SAVINGS,
AT HOME AND ABROAD

*Mr. Greenspan was puzzled about a decline in long-term interest
rates at a time of rising short-term rates, calling it a "conundrum"
that may or may not be related to a global savings glut. He returned
to the issue early in June 2005. Markets, he said, tried to push long-term
rates up early last summer and again in March this year, but in both cases
"forces came into play to make those increases short-lived. But what are those
forces? Clearly, they are not operating solely in the United States."*

From "Remarks by Chairman Alan Greenspan to the
International Monetary Conference," Beijing,
People's Republic of China, June 6, 2005.

*The individual serves the industrial system not by supplying it with
savings and the resulting capital; he serves it by consuming its products.*

John Kenneth Galbraith, *The New Industrial State* [1967].

Alan Greenspan had suffered through a year of frustration. Despite
nine fed funds rate target increases by the end of June 2005, the yield
on the key benchmark bond had *decreased*, defying not gravity but,
inexplicably, Greenspan. He initially didn't admit to knowing the cause
of such contrary behavior, so he deployed another memorable term—
it was a "conundrum." Ben Bernanke, a former Governor now at the
President's Council of Economic Advisors and a candidate to replace
the maestro, had already referred to an "unconventional" view: The
conundrum could be explained by "a global savings glut." Greenspan

did not reject this explanation but considered it to be only one of many, including a shortfall in global business investment—again, as ever, leaving his options open.

A "savings glut" *is* unconventional in the world of Adam Smith and J.B. Say, a conundrum with a capital "C." Such an admission is greatly damaging to the ideology underlying the Wall Street-Greenspan-neoconservative doctrine, according to which savings automatically create real business investment and economic growth. The interest rate comes into play because its movement is supposed to maintain a balance between savings and investment. Since the super-rich can afford to save much more, any denial of the moral force of thrift is hazardous to the mental health of the financial community.

Consider what (nearly Sir) Alan Greenspan had learned from Lord John Maynard Keynes, only soon to reject it. In an overall economy absent international trade and finance, measured saving and investment are always equal but uninterestingly so: They are equal by definition. The value of national income equals the value of what is sold or the value of all that is produced. If the value of consumption is subtracted from national income, what is not consumed is saved. If the value of consumption is subtracted from the value of what is produced and sold, that must be the value of investment in capital goods or what producers bought from each other to produce goods for consumption. Since national income is equal to the value of national output, in the overall economy measured saving and investment are equal.

The Keynesian Paradox of Thrift

Earlier we mentioned an apparent paradox uncovered by Keynes: Household savings are good for the household at most times but bad for an overall economy most of the time. Though he did not do so, Keynes' idea can be extended to the global economy. By households and businesses *intending* to save more (spend less), collectively they end up saving less. Why less? Less consumption (more personal savings) by households mean less sales for businesses and less retained earnings (business savings). Moreover, fewer capital goods bought by business firms from each other (more business savings) means less sales for businesses producing capital goods. Lower demand all the way round means fewer workers employed, less income for workers, lower profits, and a smaller national income out which workers and entrepreneurs could save. Though Keynes did not use the term, many have referred to his "paradox of thrift." It is an uncomfortable paradox for Wall Street and hedge funds because uniquely their revenues and incomes come from savings.

Conundrums begin to pile up rather quickly and awkwardly because John Maynard Keynes provides a window to a global savings glut, though not necessarily how it might be related to long-term interest rate misbehavior. An economy open to trade can reveal measured savings in excess of measured investment within the economy, as well as measured consumption in excess of what is measured within an economy (negative savings) because they both can spill over into other countries. Thus, what is normally hidden within an economy—the imbalance from what people *intend* to do—is revealed to a broader world as an excess. And, so it is. Mr. Bernanke, a neoconservative at heart, by suggesting a "global savings glut" has unwittingly stumbled into the global reality of liberal Keynesianism. Not so surprisingly, Mr. Greenspan has been nimbly dancing around such an explanation for his "conundrum" to save his revered but threatened ideology.

The World: A Glutton for Savings?

When the goods and services exports of countries such as China or Japan exceed their imports they also are exporting their "excess savings." The value of what producers within the country are producing exceeds the value of what its households and producers are buying, the residual being savings. In recent decades, those countries growing the fastest are the trade surplus countries; we have to wonder why. Within those countries, households and some businesses apparently are saving more than all their businesses want to invest. Otherwise the savings would stay at home.

The current account surpluses of Japan, the eurozone, Denmark, Norway and Sweden rose some sixty-seven percent between 1996 and 2004. The rest of the world's current account moved from a *deficit* of $99 billion to a surplus of $329 billion, an incredible swing of $428 billion. The emerging market economies are responsible for this shift; they had been running deficits prior to the currency crises of 1997–1998. Through its current account deficits (buying abroad more than it sells abroad) the United States has adsorbed about three-quarters of the "surplus savings" of the world. From those "borrowings" Americans have been able to buy more and more foreign goods (and some services) as substitutes for American goods and services. Some of the goods bought by Americans are purchased because they are cheaper, such as electronics from China and Southeastern Asian; some are bought because they are quality luxury goods such as Lexus or BMW autos. A portion of what the United States imports, of course, is comprised of commodities (Canada and the Middle East) and capital (Germany) for further production. Unwittingly, at least as a nation, the United States has become the buyer of last resort in the global economy.

Still another apparent paradox exists when we extend Keynes' own paradox to the global economy. If Americans were not spending more than they were producing, Chinese and other households and businesses *would not have* surplus savings to send back (recycle as loans) to us. American expenditures for goods are generating surplus foreign savings! In part, this imbalance is related to highly unequal income and wealth distributions that are mirrored in the American experience but with different consequences. The peasants in China may want to consume more but have insufficient incomes; the entrepreneurs in Beijing spend as fast as they can but still have funds left over that can be used to buy not only luxury goods but IBM and GE stock. China's central bank buys U.S. dollars (U.S. Treasuries) to keep its own currency cheap (lowering the external value of the yuan) and, by extension, its exports cheap, to further enhance its trade surplus.

The American wage earner cannot afford to buy most goods produced in the U.S. so they buy Chinese "Take-Out" from Wal-Mart, produced by even cheaper Chinese labor at a low-valued yuan. Since the Asian and other currency crises as well as the bursting of the Great American Stock Bubble, near-zero interest rates combined with equity loans and credit card debt has sustained a U.S. growth in

Keynesian-style effective demand that, except for financial services, has been mostly external. Ironically, even this has been subsidized by the huge Bush II tax cuts that have supported luxury goods purchases by the rich and super-rich. Private debt has done for poor and middle class Americans what public debt has done for rich Americans. In turn, many of the loans, both private and public, have been made to the U.S. by other nations.

Not only do Americans live in a Keynesian world necessitating the odd couple of large federal budget deficits and low interest rates to avoid depression-level unemployment, so do people in Japan and the eurozone. The emerging nations depend on America's private credit economy (indebted consumers) for their continued expansion. Much of this Keynesian deficiency has come from the frightening effects of the Internet and tech crashes. Low confidence levels have corroded the impulse to invest in real plant and equipment in the U.S., as well as in much of the rest of the world. It is easier to seek returns in financial instruments, even if hedge funds must be sought as the last refuge of scoundrels seeking high returns. It is far easier to trade pieces of paper and key strokes than to build a new oil refinery or a textile factory, especially since the entrepreneur isn't sure that wage earners have sufficient incomes to buy the gasoline or the clothes. Since the giant stock market bubble burst, this instinct has not changed—that is, the instinct to buy assets—it has only shifted somewhat toward upscale or luxury primary, vacation and second homes.

The danger Keynes poses for the neoconservative hegemony is double-edged because a spender caught in the act is not saving. Demand creating the need to produce and to somehow maintain the purchasing power of the working class, is critical to economic growth and full employment. Alan Greenspan and any copycat are not the central bankers who will recognize this Keynesian reality. Rather, Greenspan likely will be leaving his post in the wake of an expanding housing bubble that will only temporarily fill the vacuum left by the bursting of the Nasdaq bubble. While Keynes comes closer to the truth regarding real investment causing real saving, he nonetheless leaves an incomplete explanation of financial asset inflation and its effect on the real economy. On an important, even crucial, matter affecting the financial wealth holders as well as ordinary people, Smith, Greenspan and Keynes were wrongheaded. We concede Keynes one point; we correctly measure real saving as the value of real investment in a country *and* the global economy. The world economy has not really saved unless it has a new factory, equipment or highway to show for it.

The "Angels' Share" of Savings and Wall Street's Heavenly Returns

If personal (household) and business savings do not end as real investment, in the cloistered world of economists they play no further economic role. Yet, during the 1980s, when money and bonds were thrown, in giant bundles, at rich people, net fixed investment (the really real part of investment because it excludes depreciation) sharply declined. Most important, the growth rates of capital services in the private business and manufacturing sectors had almost fallen through the factory floor by 1985–1988. During the 1980s, the one thing private business did best was depreciation—lose capital to wear, tear, obsolescence, and destruction. Investment's counterpart, personal savings as commonly measured, continued to be meager during the bullish 1990s. Why—in an age when the idolatry of capital has never been greater and the incomes (and surely personal savings) of the virtually tax-free super-rich ascending—did so many machines commit suicide?

In the meaning ordinarily used by economists, savings evaporated. In the vineyards of France, the angels' share of cognac is the needed amount evaporated to give cognac its celebrated quality. The wine makers think that the seasonal amount evaporated equals all the cognac consumed in France during the year, sufficient to keep many spirits high. In like fashion, most of the personal savings of the wealth holders did evaporate; I have called it the "angels' share" of savings. Since Wall Street is addicted to these personal savings, the great evaporated amount must be sufficient—from the Wall Street-Greenspan-neoconservative view— to maintain the celebrated quality of Wall Street capitalism. In truth, Wall Street needs a rapidly expanding angels' share of savings for its prosperity.

Savings or Saving: Which Is It and Why Does It Matter?

A different and widely ignored view of savings comes from measuring income broadly. If income includes everything that contributes to personal wealth, it includes capital gains from stocks and bonds as well as wages and salaries. In this broader perspective, savings are the net additions to wealth or net worth. Therefore, if we have income from all sources (including paper or realized capital gains from stocks of $10,000) of $70,000, pay taxes of $15,000, and spend $45,000 on consumption, we have savings of $20,000. If we began the year with wealth or a net worth of $250,000, our net worth at the end of the year will be $20,000 higher or $270,000, reflecting partly the $10,000 gain in bonds. The increase in net worth is our savings defined broadly.

Not surprisingly, the official measure of savings understates personal money savings during the past quarter century. Since the U.S. Commerce Department and other nation's equivalents use the narrow definition of savings, they fail to account for changes in net worth, including that created by new credit or by capital gains. If Jenna Jones (daughter of Mother Jones, not the magazine) owns assets, such as securities that appreciate, which she sells at a comfortable profit, are those savings any less real to Jenna than savings accumulated by thrift? Yet, if Jenna uses capital gains from the sale of her bonds and buys a new car, Commerce records an increase in consumption that *reduces* personal savings. These unmeasured savings comprise part of the angels' share.

The financial wealth holders have the bulk of these personal savings. The middle class can only borrow against it. The more businesses and governments parcel out as interest payments and dividends, the greater the increases in savings by these wealth holders. Moreover, though the corporation can increase its cash from equities only with new issues (which were rare during the 1980s and 1990s), Warren Buffett's family and other wealthy households can enjoy secondary market appreciation in its equities' holdings without necessarily sharing any of those benefits with business. When 14–16 cents (net) of every new dollar of government spending goes to bondholders as interest, can anyone doubt that the net worth of those few holding bonds is rising? Ignoring capital gains, an *average* $106,000 annual risk-free yearly income from government bonds goes to the super-rich family. When the Dow doubles, can anyone doubt that the net worth of rich households has risen? The gain of the super-rich will have been more than $2 trillion (equaling about a quarter of the yearly national GDP) or an average $1.8 billion per household. Can anyone doubt that the wealth distribution becomes more unequal as the bond and stock markets soar? Those unearned income gains essentially add only to the current savings of wealth holders, and do so without making any contact whatsoever with business firms beyond brokerage houses (and Greenspan has admitted to knowing this).

Business Savings and the Angels' Share Derived From Corporations

The solution to the savings' mystery is not complete without considering why even business savings can evaporate. Business savings are conventionally measured as retained earnings of corporations and other firms, those earnings not paid out as dividends to the shareholders. As a percentage of GDP, in the U.S. they fell from around four point five percent in the mid-1960s to one percent during the late 1980s. During the decade corporations were repurchasing their own stock, raising its price, to ward off takeovers during the outbreak of leveraged buyouts, evasive actions probably explaining why corporate saving turned even lower. During 1995–1997, for similar reasons, corporations again were buying back great amounts of their own stock. In total, corporations bought back more stock than they issued, so that net issues were negative in five of the ten years 1995–2004.

There was a pause related to the end of Great Bull Market; net corporate savings soared from negative territory in the year 2000 to around two percent of GDP. Alan Greenspan himself was telling Congress on July 20, 2005 that 2003 was the first year since the recession of 1975 that U.S. companies' capital expenditures were below corporate cash flow. Red Hat Inc., the Linux software firm, spent $23 million on research, development, plant and equipment in the quarter ended May 31, 2005, but spent $15 million repurchasing its own stock and debt. J.C. Penney Co., the retailer, spent $99 million on real capital, but spent $554 million repurchasing its own stock and debt. Motorola followed a similar path with its first-ever stock-buyback program. As a share of the global GDP, companies haven't been this thrifty at any time during the past forty years, but with little real to show for it. Even oil exporters are not building refineries or buying equipment despite their recently huge windfalls.

The cash flow of American corporations is more likely to be used to inflate stock prices held by households (including, of course, the households of corporate CEOs) than to be deployed to plant and other capital. Business savings, instead of becoming real investment become capital gains (gains that are not even normally measured as savings). We arrive at a remarkable phenomenon: The growth of net worth or wealth in the American economy and many other mature economies apparently has switched from business firms to selected families. Ultimately, if companies fail to spend their earnings on capital or capital improvements, they are returned to households as higher stock prices or greater dividends. The capital gains effect of net negative business savings are transferred to households, evaporating, sadly, going the way of much of cognac, adding to the angels' share of savings. And, now, it is a global economy problem.

A Summation: The Hypocrisy of Financial Market Efficiency

The corporate deployment of its securities as a means of raising funds for new investment illustrates how easily we can slip into the Wall Street-Greenspan error of thinking that saving "causes" investment. Household savings, for instance, are sources of new corporate debt, an indebtedness no doubt incurred solely for real business investment in, as examples, construction of a new Marriott hotel or the purchase of new airplanes by Delta. However, these household savings only enter the firm when new corporate bonds are issued. Otherwise, households are merely exchanging ownership of corporate (and no doubt government) bonds with each other. Besides, though net corporate bond issues have been substantial in recent years, net new issues of corporate equities have been vanishing.

This process whereby trillions of dollars are required to maintain liquidity in financial markets generating slightly more than a hundred billion or sometimes (recently, in corporate stocks) negative amounts of funds seems highly inefficient. Even the market heralded as the "most efficient," the U.S. Treasuries market, required an average of two thousand seven hundred and two trades a day and $45.8 trillion in secondary market activity in 1994 to yield only $185.3 billion for the Treasury. In short, the value of re-sales of securities was two hundred and forty-seven times the value of funds raised! A labor market working this way would have to hire two hundred and forty-seven workers to do the work of one. In these highly inefficient markets, the value of financial assets is bid up and the wealth and income distributions made more lopsided.

The stock markets serve the Greenspan Standard; that is, they are the route to greater wealth for CEOs holding stock options. Since only one to four percent of the value of stock transactions raise new funds for corporations, they are not very good at serving the interests of real capitalism, only Wall Street capitalism. Otherwise, combined with an oracle at the Fed, the minute-by-minute gyrations in stock prices is simply a diversion, entertainment far more expensive than a blockbuster action movie. But, let us be fair: without stock markets the Federal Reserve chair would not have enough financial markets to crash and sufficient reasons to engage in risk management. There's always nonetheless the on-going house party: Perhaps it can be crashed.

19

KING ALAN II

Now, we come to wonder. Which pair of Alan Greenspan's shoes will be filled should he decide to relinquish his chair? Will it be those of the wizard, maestro, Pope of Wall Street, oracle, or of a title so exalted, it has still to be used? True, Alan Greenspan has been knighted in the United Kingdom. As an American—still beneath the dignity of former colonial masters—he couldn't be titled "sir," so unlike *Sir* Mick Jagger. If Mr. Greenspan stays on after the end of his current term, for whatever period, only "King Alan II" would suffice.

Since Greenspan has been deemed indispensable, an extension of his present term is plausible. He could be the present and future king. As late as May 2005, the White House hadn't begun a formal search of Greenspan's successor. It's "premature," White House Deputy Chief of Staff Karl Rove said that month, "It's important that the Fed chairman remain strong throughout his entire term." Republicans already had begun a search for a successor to President Bush. Alan Greenspan still appears to be indispensable.

When Greenspan does step down, the power of the head of the Federal Reserve System will have been permanently enhanced. Royal may be more descriptive of the position. Greenspan did not establish a throne alone: The Federal Reserve System has been able to exercise enormous and independent power since its restoration by President Dwight D. Eisenhower. This power will go undiminished until at least 2008 when a new President of the United States will either be elected or again appointed. As a Democrat president (Bill Clinton) ceded his entire domestic economic program to Greenspan, party affiliation has little to do with it.

The appointment of a new chair of the Reserve is not a trivial matter. By mid-year 2005 four probable candidates had emerged; all of whom had dependable Republican credentials. They were Martin S. Feldstein, R. Glenn Hubbard, Ben S. Bernanke, and Lawrence Lindsey. The following provides a heads-up on what to expect of the person who may well have been appointed by the time this chapter is printed.

If these four and Greenspan were golf balls driven off the same tee, wherein the balls represent free-market ideology, a fig leaf would cover them all. Martin Feldstein, a Harvard University economics professor and President of the prestigious National Bureau of Economic Research, is a leading candidate. At 65 he is experienced enough for the tasks at hand. Not only did Feldstein, like Greenspan, advise President Reagan but he also has been a leading advocate of Social Security private accounts as well as lower taxes for the rich and for corporations. Feldstein has a reputation as a solid, free-market economist and always has been on the side of President W's tax-cutting agenda. He sees Bush's budget deficits shrinking if the President has even reasonable control over discretionary spending (*code* for social welfare spending). He is considered a strong and "reputable" source of support for private Social Security accounts, even as he plays down the scale of benefit cuts or tax increases to maintain overall solvency. As an adviser to George W. Bush in 2000 he helped shape Mr. Bush's tax cutting priorities. Indeed, social insurance and corporate taxes (though presently near zero) are his academic specialties. Mr. Feldstein serves on corporate boards of directors, including American International Group (AIG), a giant insurance company under investigation in 2005 for possible accounting fraud.

Most recently, Mr. Feldstein has backed a Social Security proposal by House and Senate Republicans for "personal retirement accounts," the Orwellian phrase for partial privatization. Instead of surplus Social Security dollars being transferred to the general budget, the surplus dollars would be put into private accounts. As sufficiently noted, the surplus is not supposed to go into the general revenues anyway. The private accounts would "supplement" reduced pay-as-you-go benefits and after 2008 could be shifted into stock and bond mutual funds, the same funds that bought Enron, WorldCom, AIG, and other accounting-challenged corporations' stocks and bonds. There are numerous other rat holes that the social security surplus could be poured down; once

Wall Street gets its take through high salaries and sales staff overheads plus fees, nothing would be left anyway. This three-trick pony would misuse the surpluses that the Social Security system won't have, eventually destroying everything in its path except neoconservative ideology.

Worse, Mr. Feldstein, a distinguished Harvard professor who surely knows better, pulls from his shot-from-the-hip bottle, J.B. Say, pour le 100 proof coup de grace from the Frenchman. The private account supplements, Feldstein writes, "would also increase national saving," and "finance investment in plant and equipment that raises productivity and produces the extra national income to finance future retiree benefits." This alone is sufficient to take Arthur Laffer's breath away, but there are still more benefits to flow. "A higher national saving rate would also reduce dependence on capital from abroad and would therefore shrink our trade deficit." This grown-up economist is confusing personal savings with automatic real investment not only at home, but also abroad. Private accounts would accomplish everything except reducing the visibility of Paris Hilton.

R. Glenn Hubbard, about 20 years younger than Feldstein, also specializes in corporate finance and taxes as well as money and banking. He was Deputy Assistant Treasury Secretary for Tax, 1991–1993 and Chairman of George W's Council of Economic Advisers, 2001–2003. He too vigorously supported Mr. Bush's priorities of creating private accounts and cutting taxes of the rich and of corporations. His pet project was the promotion of the 2003 tax cuts that included corporate dividends. He and Greenspan disagree on the effects of federal budget deficits on interest rates; Hubbard's research finds no link between the two. For further insight into Mr. Hubbard, we can read his columns in *Business Week* in its tri-weekly rotation to a conservative economist. In January 2005 he writes that the Fed, not Pillsbury, "wisely insulated from the political process," deserves a "gold medal" for achieving price stability. After leaving the Bush White House, Hubbard moved on to be dean of Columbia University's graduate business school.

Ben Bernanke, about half a decade older than Hubbard, is a former Fed governor (2000–2005), who is chairman of the Council of Economic Advisers (CEA), a White House position once held by the other two men and by, yes, Mr. Greenspan. Bernanke taught monetary policy and econometrics at Princeton University before going to the Fed in 2000. He is outspoken, wears a beard and is very casual for a "serious" central banker. He once said that his most difficult part of being at the Reserve was wearing a suit. Still, his speech-making and heavy research agenda gave him prominence at the Fed. He nonetheless suffers another flaw: while chairman of Princeton's economics department, he hired star economist Paul Krugman, who has since become a vigorous Bush critic on any issue anyone would care to name. In Bernanke's favor to head the Fed, he is, like Alan Greenspan, a libertarian Republican.

In July 2005, as the new chairman of the CEA, Bernanke gave a speech to the American Enterprise Institute, a favorite refuge for central bankers, which would provide comfort to the Bush administration. He assured us that "We are in the midst of a healthy and sustainable economic expansion," and inflation should remain low. While "speculative behavior appears to be surfacing in some local [housing] markets," the Bush administration will "monitor these developments," but the best defense against problems are "vigilant lenders and borrowers." Bernanke shares Greenspan's reluctance to restrain rapidly rising asset markets. He said little about President Bush's proposed private Social Security accounts. Rising tax revenue should lead to a federal budget deficit below the $427 billion earlier projected. He also said—and this certainly fits the Wall Street-Greenspan financial markets strategy and Say's law fetish—there is some evidence of a beneficial "supply side" bounce to the president's tax cuts on income, capital gains and dividends since people are working more and businesses are investing more when these activities are taxed less. As noted, wives certainly are working more. Mr. Bernanke, like Feldstein and Hubbard, is unlikely to keep interest rates low if inflation raises it ugly head.

Lawrence Lindsey, a consulting economist and Mr. Feldstein's former student, was a Fed governor from 1991 to 1997. His was the strongest voice warning of the dangers of the late 1990s stock market bubble. An adviser to President Bush during his 2000 campaign and as director of the White House National Economic Council, he remains a strong advocate of lower taxes for the wealthy. Like his former professor, Lindsey is a devotee of supply-side economics and the belief that economic growth is spurred by tax cuts for the rich. He shares these beliefs with Vice President Dick Cheney who is heading the search for a new Fed chairman. We could not get an opinion from Cheney; he is at an "undisclosed location."

All the candidates, Bernanke included, favor zero or near-zero goods inflation. In that respect, they are as one with many central bankers around the world. In short, the leading candidates for Greenspan's job are ideological comrades. Hubbard and Lindsey, to their credit, contend that asset bubbles can exist and that they do create problems. Hubbard, however, has proposed no remedy. We turn, finally, to prospects for reform, not only of the central bank but of other institutions.

20

PROSPECTS FOR REFORM

A plethora of measures to reform central banks exist, though most come from a distant past. Free market fundamentalism—Alan Greenspan, neoconservatives, financial "experts," and giant multinational financial enterprises—have held sway for more than a quarter century. Although optimism is a valuable trait, it never guarantees that reason will prevail. Reform, we would judge, awaits a time when The Market is no longer God, when blemishes such as the mountains on the moon and spots on the sun first seen by Galileo, create modest doubts about the perfection of free market Heaven and by association, the deification of Mr. Greenspan and his successors. Doubt, as if creeping on little cat paws through the moon glow, will then erode thoughtless faith. Reform will require all of this, and perhaps more.

Conventional wisdom, as John Kenneth Galbraith defines it, is "approved belief." Where faith redounds to personal or group financial benefits, we find therein few realists but many innocent hypocrites—even in American literature. Because of his profound faith in wealth Jay Gatsby heard only the sound of money in Daisy Buchanan's voice. If he had been a realist, he would have known that Daisy, who had married "old" wealth, would have a faith that ran even deeper than his. She had not only wealth but all the legitimate power that it embodied by virtue of its age. With *The Great Gatsby* and other novels, F. Scott Fitzgerald ultimately not only defined the Jazz age, but unmasked the corrupting influence of wealth.

Minds are not easily changed. The smoothly efficient market, especially since it doesn't exist, is a haven from cruel reality. It is far better to go to the latest movie on hurricanes than to try to explain their mysterious forces. Just as we are reluctant to believe what a one hundred and forty-mile-an-hour wind can do to our beachfront second home

160

until it blows us away, finance specialists are equally reluctant to predict disaster especially if it is eminent. As we have seen, not only did Alan Greenspan claim not to be able to identify bubbles, he says that he could have done nothing about them until they burst in his face, then only to do the wrong thing.

Literature may not be a bad place to begin. Greenspan's concern that literature continue to be taught in universities is a basis for some agreement. *The Great Gatsby* remains a cautionary tale of the eternal pitfalls for those morally blinded by money and wealth. When "public servants" innocently or purposefully pursue policies benefiting mostly the rich, they ultimately serve neither the rich nor poor. Jeb Bush, President W's brother, had $2.1 million in net worth in 1999 before he had to put $1.6 million in a blind trust as the elected Governor of Florida; by 2005 the value of his blind trust had dropped to $798,000, the biggest losses coming when the stock market went south, even of Florida.

There is poetic justice in restoring Robin Hood to his rightful if literary moral place of taking from the rich to give to the poor, making both better off. His name should not, as has become recent neo-conservative practice, be sullied in defense of greater tax cuts for the wealthy—pitied for being the downtrodden. Zorro, Spain's version of Robin Hood, if alive as well as realistic, would today be defending Latino agricultural workers and workers in the sweatshops. But, to take those actions today, Zorro would still have to disguise himself, hide by day, and act by night. If he were then to testify before the U.S. Joint Economic Committee of Congress, he would be ill-advised to remove his mask. Moving away from the Greenspan Standard will not be easy.

Pursuit of Reform at the Federal Reserve

In the U.S., we could try to make the Federal Reserve more responsible to the Congress through the Joint Economic Committee. Unfortunately this committee presently is in the throes of neoconservatism and is unlikely to vote against its own ideology. So, we return full circle to ideology, which surely will soon be confronted with reality. Prudent judgment moderated by reality recommends that the Federal Reserve

System somehow be made more responsible to the body politic without taking away the Fed's operating efficiency. Reforms that could accomplish this would generally enhance congressional and White House authority.

I have recommended giving the Joint Economic Committee of Congress authority to set up a watchdog committee, a Congressional Monetary Committee (CMC), comprising academic and technical experts who would evaluate monetary policy on a continuous basis. The responsibilities of the CMC would be comparable to the federal tax analysis now provided by the bipartisan Joint Tax Committee of Congress and the federal budget analysis of the bipartisan Congressional Budget Office. To add force to the recommendations of the CMC, we should give the Joint Economic Committee itself direct authority to appoint two of the seven Governors, while the five regional Reserve Bank presidents serving on the Board of Governors would be removed. If nonetheless neoconservative academics and "experts" are appointed to such a committee, life will go on as usual, again highlighting the importance of moving away from the current neoconservative ideology.

Cooling the Ardor of Speculators

Long-term capital gains—gains taking place over several years—have long been considered the flywheel of capitalism. Rare is the economist who finds long-term capital gains undesirable. Quick capital gains on secondary financial instruments are of a different character; generally, the purpose of such sudden sales is to make money on money, something accomplished in a time too brief and too indirect to produce real capital. If we prefer lasting to fleeting capitalism, excessive speculative gains are to be discouraged.

A transactions tax recommends itself for particular kinds of domestic financial transfers. The recently revitalized thirty-year bond, for example, was not designed to change hands daily. It, and ten-year bonds, was intended to provide funds for long-term, real investment. Fixed rate mortgages for financing housing is an example that comes easily to mind. Even equities originally were considered "long-term capital investments" both because perpetual corporations used them to provide finance for new factories and because households held them such a long time. A properly designed financial transactions tax would discourage speculation in securities. Such a tax, sufficient to sting but not so great as to eliminate adequate gains, would be directed at the new leisure class of speculators, who have increased financial market volatility and made speculation more lucrative.

Any person or institution buying and selling General Motors or any other stock in less than a year have either been imprudent in their purchasing decision or are speculating. A transactions tax, graduated from a high percentage near term and vaporizing at the end of a year's holding period, would discourage short-term speculation in the stock markets. A similar tax could be applied to financial derivatives based upon stocks and bonds. The Clinton Administration manifested an awareness of the importance of longer holding periods for financial investments. The 1997 capital gains tax law lowered the top rate from twenty to eighteen percent for assets purchased and held at least five years. Those with incomes less than $41,200 (joint filers) enjoyed a capital gains tax rate of only ten percent for eighteen-month assets and eight percent for five-year holdings. Unfortunately, households at this income level do not hold sufficient values of securities to merit taxation. The further design of such a tax itself should be subject to long-term study.

A Restoration (Somehow) of Fiscal Policy: The Role of Interest-Free Loans for Infrastructure

Lost in the quagmire of ideology is the Keynesian idea that orchestrated changes in federal expenditures and revenues could be used to stabilize the economy and to influence economic growth. The loss of fiscal policy is not uniquely American; it has been abandoned in the U.K. and elsewhere. Monetary policy emerged as the sole national economic policy out of academic obsession and ideologically convenience. Even at its best, monetary policy can't do all the heavy lifting. In its bias against goods inflation and the wages of working people to favor asset inflation, it contributes to an inequality requiring government spending (at some level), unless a society chooses to ignore the welfare of its most vulnerable citizens.

Tax-supported bodies—state, local and provincial governments—should be able to borrow money, *interest-free*, directly from their national treasuries for capital projects and for paying off existing debt. Such loans—*not* grants—would be for capital projects only, *not* day-to-day expenses. For example, public schools could borrow to build new classrooms but not to pay teachers. Such investments are in need of stimulation, especially in the U.S. and the U.K. Furthermore, public investment has very high rates of return because it stimulates economic growth and employment as better highways, schools, airports, and cleaner water boost the output and sales of private industry. Public capital investment stimulates private investment. The idea of interest-free loans seems to be catching on in the United States.

Interest-free loans could be the basis for a flexible, new fiscal policy. Just as with golf swings, timing is vital; the treasury could introduce interest-free bonds during economic recessions or periods of slow economic growth. Though counter-cyclical timing of the amounts of new issues of interest-free bonds could resurrect fiscal policy, its effectiveness, like the success of low interest rates during the financing of World War II, would require the cooperation of central banks. With a central bank's cooperation (or reform measures to guarantee its support), the timing of new issues of such bonds during recessions could increase employment without adding to the federal budget deficit or to the national debt.

Progressive Taxes and the Business Cycle

Though monetary reforms are critical, true tax reform is an essential counterpart in the restoration of economic well-being on Main Street. We have seen how deficit finance as a substitute for progressive tax finance gives windfall gains to the wealth holders while hurting everyone else. Meanwhile, the tax burden of the working class has steadily increased with each increase in social security tax payments. Not only has the income tax system become ever more regressive (with higher rates applying to lower incomes), it has become an inadequate source of general revenue. The federal government has transferred ever more necessary fiscal burdens to state and local governments that have always relied on regressive taxes.

The more successful a financial transactions tax in slowing speculation, the less government revenue it will yield. If we want a federal investment budget and we want to keep the current revenue and expenses budget roughly balanced over the course of the business cycle, the nation needs an enhanced tax base, only part of which could come from a faster economic growth pace. Besides, as I have said, an over-reliance on deficit finance from tax cuts for very rich households tilts income and wealth toward the top of the pyramid.

Irrespective of the exact tax structure, there are many advantages from making income taxes more progressive. First, truly progressive taxation alone would provide a built-in automatic stabilizer that the U.S. and the U.K. once enjoyed. When business activity slows, tax revenues would automatically slow, reducing any budget surplus or causing a budget deficit, and therefore off-setting declines in private consumption, housing construction or real business investment. A progressive income tax assures that those poor and middle income families falling into lower tax rate brackets would be spending more, for what they spend is on household necessities. When the economy is growing rapidly, rising tax revenues can prevent the growth from being overly exuberant. Second, historically lopsided income and wealth distributions always have led to speculative excesses, a rise in the angels' share of savings, financial crises, and, more often than not, great economic disruptions. Tax revenue from savings that otherwise evaporate could be redeployed as capital infrastructure to speed real economic growth.

An Incomes Policy: Beyond Ideological Blindness

Besides the need for a new tax base, countries also need a means to fight inflation other than central bank's twin sledgehammers—reduced credit and high interest rates—designed as they are to beat an economy into submission. When employment and lower incomes for workers must be exchanged for "price stability," it is a Faustian bargain. Though goods inflation has not been a problem in the industrialized world for more than a quarter century, even relative price stability and the prospect for worldwide deflation have not prevented Alan Greenspan and other central bankers from continuing to fight the ghost of inflations past. Dickens' Scrooge, before Christmas enlightenment, would be proud.

There is no shortage of details regarding tax reform and an incomes policy elsewhere. Embedded in these reforms is a new kind of incomes policy that would use tax incentives to limit wage and profits inflation, making it unnecessary to use monetary policy to cause recession and slow growth to limit goods inflation. The income tax system could be simplified with only three progressive tax rates; additional revenue could be derived from a value added tax (already deployed in most industrialized nations). The value added tax provides an ideal tax device for a new kind of incomes policy. At the same time conservatives could be given a kind of tax they have long sought; a value added tax favors real investment at the expense of some consumption. It could provide welcome tax revenue if its regressive effects are offset by enhancing tax credits already existing.

A Final Word or Two

There is nothing inherently wrong about income and wealth inequalities. It would be a mistake to make such a world flat; income differences can be a productivity motivator. We are concerned with the *degree* of massive inequalities that can't be justified on either economic or moral grounds and therefore require irrational and ideological defenses. John Maynard Keynes long ago tried to draw this line—to demark needed inequalities. Once the source of real private investment is understood, Keynes concludes, "our argument leads towards the conclusion that in contemporary conditions the growth of wealth, so far from being dependent on the abstinence of the rich, as is commonly supposed, is more likely to be impeded by it." And, he adds, "one of the chief social justifications of great inequality of wealth is, therefore, removed." He realized, of course, that other arguments could be made, but "for my own part, I believe that there is social and psychological justification for significant inequalities of incomes and wealth, but not for such large disparities as exist today." Today those inequalities are obscene worldwide. Such extraordinary wealth differences also add to asset price volatility and encourage the proliferation of risky derivatives.

There is no shortage of reform proposals with merit. What is to be encouraged is enlightenment ascending beyond the IQ and sensitivity of the grammar school bully. We can move toward reasoned reform, especially in the richest nation, one built first only on hope. We can remain optimistic that neoconservative extremism, especially its abrasive meanness, is coming to an end. Otherwise, citizens of the world should tremble.

NOTES

(numbers on leftmost margin refer to page numbers)

Note for page x

x Similarly, William McChesney Martin Jr., the chairman from 1951 to 1970, was appointed by President Truman (Dem.) but was reappointed by Presidents Eisenhower (Rep.), Kennedy (Dem.), Johnson (Dem.), and Nixon (Rep.). Paul Volcker (Dem.), the chairman from 1979 to 1987, was appointed by President Carter (Dem.) but was reappointed by President Reagan (Rep.).

Notes for pages 6–7

6 Quoted by Ayn Rand's biographer, Barbara Branden, *The Passion of Ayn Rand* (Garden City: Doubleday & Company, 1986), p. 132.

6 *Newsweek*, February 24, 1974. A very similar quote is attributed to the *New York Times* by Steven K. Beckner, *Back From the Brink: The Greenspan Years* (New York: John Wiley and Sons, 1996), p. 12. Beckner first became acquainted with Greenspan through his writings on the virtues of laissez-faire economics and the gold standard in Ayn Rand's journal. Later, Beckner covered Greenspan as a financial journalist in Washington. For the most part, Beckner's book is laudatory, though what Beckner praises Greenspan for, others might condemn him.

7 Quoted in Barbara Branden, *The Passion of Ayn Rand* (New York: Doubleday, 1986), p. 292.

Notes for pages 10–15

10   Quoted by Eleanora Schoenebaum, *Political Profiles: The Nixon/Ford Years* (New York: Facts on File, 1979), p. 252.

11   "Health, Education, Income Security and Social Services," 9/19/74 bound transcript, L. William Seidman files, Box 6, Gerald Ford Presidential Library.

11   See Beckner, *op. cit.*, p. 15.

11   Alan Greenspan, Testimony Before the Senate Judiciary Committee, U.S. Congress, June 16, 1998.

14   Adam Smith, *An Inquiry into the Nature and Causes of the Wealth of Nations*, edited by Edwin Cannan, with an introduction by Max Lerner (New York: Modern library, 1937) [1776], p. 321.

15   Adam Smith's ideas are misused by those who invoke his name against government provisions of important public goods and services. If we ever met Smith, we would agree that Alan Greenspan is no Adam Smith. Overall, Smith favored government provision of military security, the administration of justice, and privately unprofitable public works and instructions. When we turn to specifics, the list runs to fifteen items, among which are the government's right to impose tariffs to counter tariffs, to punish business fraud, to regulate banking, to provide post offices, highways, harbors, bridges and canals, and so on. Even so, only if private domestic markets were unfettered would the consumer continue to reign as king. For the same reason, Smith also opposed monopolization of the production of a commodity. The radical free-marketeers, however, came long after Adam Smith, who would have opposed the merger movement of the past quarter-century.

Notes for pages 18–25

18   For the view that even bubbles are rational, see Yangru Wu, "Rational Bubbles in the Stock Market: Accounting for the

U.S. Stock-Price Volatility," *Economic Enquiry*, April 1997, pp. 309–319. For a critique of "rational bubbles" and a historical view of manias, see E. Ray Canterbery, "Irrational Exuberance and Rational Speculative Bubbles," Presidential Address to the International Trade and Finance Association, *The International Trade Journal*, Summer 1999.

20   The full content of Greenspan's letter can be found as Appendix C of Martin Mayer, *The Greatest-Ever Bank Robbery: The Collapse of the Savings and Loan Industry* (New York: Macmillan Publishing Company, 1990). A full reading of the letter will inspire little trust in Greenspan's regulatory leadership. A dedicated reader of Mayer's book will come away with a complete understanding of what happened to the savings & loan industry, and why. See, too, Martin Mayer, *The Bankers: The Next Generation* (New York: Truman Talley Books/Dutton, 1997), chapter 12.

20   From testimony of Patricia S. McJoynt, senior vice-president of the Federal Home Loan Bank of Seattle, October 31, 1989, before the House Banking Committee, in Investigation of Lincoln Savings & Loan Association (Washington, D.C.: U.S. Government Printing Office, 1989), part 3, p. 160.

21   Quote is from the delayed Transcript, Federal Open Market Committee Meeting, August 18, 1987, p. 24. Like President Richard M. Nixon when in the White House, the FOMC had secretly tape-recorded its meetings, an act admitted by Greenspan in 1993. Public officials then began demanding that the Reserve release transcripts. After enough foot-dragging by Greenspan to have impaired his tennis game, the Reserve finally agreed to release "lightly edited" transcripts of its meetings, with a five-year lag.

21   Quoted by Bob Woodward, *Maestro: Greenspan's Fed and the American Boom* (Simon & Schuster: New York, 2000), p. 28, from one of "more than 100 sources who agreed to provide information as long as their identities would not be revealed" (p. 256).

21   Quote is from Woodward, *Ibid.*, p. 33.

23   Quote is from Woodward, *Ibid.*, p. 47.

23   *Ibid.* The interplay between Corrigan and Greenspan is told in great detail in Woodward, *Ibid.*, pp. 38–42.

24   Dr. Greenspan has always been very protective of his chairmanship. Although vice chairman Johnson was a logical choice to succeed Greenspan in 1990, Johnson's moves would have been viewed as "arrogant" by a chairman determined to remain in office. Wall Street insiders, members of Congress and the next President of the United States would know about this infraction as well as Johnson's exuberance for economic growth and insufficient fear of goods inflation. Johnson resigned August 3, 1990.

25   Woodward, *op. cit.*, p. 72. For more details on the Citibank rescue, see Woodward, *Ibid.*, pp. 72–73.

Notes for pages 30–34

30   These quotes come from statements on the purposes and functions of the Federal Reserve, by and for, the Federal Reserve (*www.federalreserve.gov/generalinfo*). No women has ever served as chair and apparently the current Board of Governors does not expect any gender changes any time soon because "chairman" is used throughout these statements.

32   Today the Federal Reserve Banks discount U.S. Treasury bills, the Treasury's short-maturity debt, held by private commercial banks.

34   Quotes are from a speech by Alan Greenspan at the Washington Hilton, sponsored by the American Enterprise Institute for Public Policy Research, December 5, 1996.

Notes for pages 37–42

37   See John Kenneth Galbraith, *The Economics of Innocent Fraud* (Boston/New York: Houghton Mifflin, 2004).

39   These various M's were invented by economists at the Federal Reserve. For the details on how and why these aggregate money supplies were developed, see E. Ray Canterbery, *Wall Street*

Capitalism (World Scientific: Singapore/New Jersey, 2000), pp. 76–83.

40   "Minutes of the Federal Open Market Committee," June 29–30, 2005, *www.federal reserve.gov/fomc/minutes.*

42   Board of Governors of the Federal Reserve System, 89th Annual Report (Washington, D.C.: Board of Governors of the Federal Reserve System, 2002), pp. 281–282, 309–310, 318–319.

Notes for pages 47–50

47   See E. Ray Canterbery, *Wall Street Capitalism* (Singapore/New Jersey: World Scientific, 2000), pp. 52–54.

48   Bob Woodward, *The Agenda: Inside the Clinton White House* (New York: Simon & Schuster, 1994), p. 69.

48   *Ibid.*, p. 82.

49   *Ibid.*, p. 84.

49   *Ibid.*

49   *Ibid.*, p. 91.

49   *Ibid.*, p. 98.

50   *Ibid.*, p. 165.

50   Robert Reich, *Locked in the Cabinet* (New York: Alfred A. Knopf, 1997), p. 105.

Notes for pages 53–60

53   As quoted by Robert Reich, *Locked in the Cabinet* (New York: Alfred A. Knopf, 1997), p. 207.

53   *Ibid.*, pp. 213–214.

54   Greenspan quotes are from Transcript, Federal Open Market Committee Meeting, May 17, 1994.

55   Quoted by Louis Uchitelle, "No. 2 at Fed Tells Clinton He Is Leaving," *The New York Times*, January 17, 1996, pp. C1, C3.

56   Economists generally have missed this concordance, the way that both Smith and Keynes attribute savings and real investment to separate people.

58   The reader can find much more about Adam Smith, John Maynard Keynes, Milton Friedman, and many other famous economists in E. Ray Canterbery, *A Brief History of Economics* (New Jersey/London/Singapore: World Scientific, 2001). For still more detail on Smith and Keynes as well as the history of their times, see Canterbery, *The Making of Economics, 4ᵗʰ Edition, Vol. I* (New Jersey/London/Singapore: World Scientific, 2003).

60   At the time the natural rate of unemployment was a rate at which any further expansionary policies causes inflation without any further reductions in the unemployment rate. For a detailed critique of the 1997 *Economic Report of the President*, see James K. Galbraith, "The Clinton Administration's Vision," *Challenge*, July–August 1997, pp. 45–57.

60   The natural rate of unemployment had mutated over time into the non-accelerating-inflation rate of unemployment (NAIRU). The relation between inflation and unemployment is roughly the same except that the "acceleration" in inflation becomes more important than the *level* of inflation.

60   Once again, for details on the contents of the 1998 *Economic Report of the President*, as well as an explanation for why falling computer prices did not alter the inflationary environment, as claimed by the Clinton economists, see James K. Galbraith, "The Economic Report of the President for 1998: A Review," *Challenge*, September–October 1998, pp. 87–98.

Note for page 65

65   These dollar estimates are gleaned from Susanne Craig and Dennis K. Berman, "Morgan Stanley To-Do List: Get Strategy, Boss," *Wall Street Journal*, June 14, 2005, pp. C1, C3. Fred Seegal, the investment banker at Stephens Inc. who represented Dean Witter in the original Morgan Stanley deal in 1997, is the source for Morgan Stanley's rates of return.

Notes for pages 70–72

70   *The Story of Monetary Policy* (New York: Federal Reserve Bank of New York, 1996). This *is* a comic book published by the New York Fed, but not the only one.

70   This fable is updated from one based only on the 1990s experiences in E. Ray Canterbery, *Wall Street Capitalism* (Singapore/New Jersey: World Scientific, 2000), Chapter 1.

72   Quotation from a Bridge News release written by Phil Serafino, May 4, 1997.

72   Quotation from an AP release written by John Hendren, May 12, 1997.

72   Quotation from a New York AP release on June 13, 1997.

Notes for pages 78–79

78   Household incomes are based on IRS data updated by Thomas Piketty and Emmanuel Saez from their article, "Income Inequality in the United States, 1913–1998," *Quarterly Journal of Economics* 118 (2003), 1–39. Because of under-reporting of income at the top, IRS data has historically understated income inequalities.

78   For much more on the changing relative fortunes of the financial wealth holders and the working class during the 1980s and 1990s, see E. Ray Canterbery, *Wall Street Capitalism* (New Jersey/London/Singapore: World Scientific, 2000).

79   The data is from the 1995 Survey of Consumer Finances by the Federal Reserve System, a survey that Alan Greenspan and the other Governors have apparently ignored or considered irrelevant. See "Family Finances in the U.S.: Recent Evidence from the Survey of Consumer Finances," *Federal Reserve Bulletin*, January 1997, pp. 1–24.

79   The 2001 wealth data are from *Federal Reserve Bulletin*, January 2003, pp. 13–19.

79   The more detailed data on wealth or net worth is from the Panel Study of Income Dynamics and is reported by Asena

Caner and Edward Wolff, "The Tragedy of Asset Poverty in the U.S.," *Challenge: The Magazine of Economic Affairs*, January–February 2004, p. 13. Wealth is such an important but overlooked indicator of economic well-being that Wolff and Caner suggest the importance of an asset poverty measure for the United States. Even a small amount of assets enables a family to weather unexpected unemployment and a drop in wages. Wolff and Caner develop a measure of such poverty in this article.

Notes for pages 84–89

84 The day was Tuesday, September 8, 1998. The percentage gain of four point nine eight percent, however, was only the 58th largest ever in percentage terms.

87 Quoted by Anita Raghavan and Mitchell Pacell, "A Hedge Fund Falters, So the Fed Beseeches Big Banks to Ante Up," *Wall Street Journal*, September 24, 1998, p. A1.

88 From Alan Greenspan's testimony, Banking Committee, U.S. House of Representatives, October 1, 1998.

88 "A Talk with Treasury Chief Rubin," *Business Week*, October 12, 1998, p. 126.

89 See the interview with McDonough in "Mr. McDonough, You Have the Floor: The Accounting Watchdog on Sarbanes-Oxley, Excessive Auditing, and Investor Trust," *Business Week*, August 1, 2005, p. 56.

Notes for pages 94–98

94 Quotes are from Alan Greenspan's testimony, Humphrey-Hawkins report on monetary policy, U.S. Congress, July 18, 1996.

96 There are too many holes in Greenspan's "theory" of the causes of the Great Depression, including the international trade and payments imbalances, to fill in less than thirty pages. My favorite take on the subject is found in E. Ray Canterbery, *A Brief History of Economics* (Singapore/New Jersey: World Scientific, 2000), Chapter 10 and, for more details, E. Ray Canterbery,

The Making of Economics, 4th Edition, Vol. I (Singapore/New Jersey: World Scientific, 2003), Chapters 11 and 12.

98   See E. Ray Canterbery, *Wall Street Capitalism* (Singapore/New Jersey: World Scientific, 2000).

Notes for pages 104–107

104   The complete story behind this legislation is told in an entertaining way by Martin Mayer, *The Fed: The Inside Story of How the World's Most Powerful Financial Institution Drives the Markets* (New York/London: The Free Press, 2001), pp. 44–52. The balance of Mayer's book also is recommended reading.

105   Quotes are from "Bonds: So Long, Easy Plays," *Business Week*, December 28, 1998, pp. 158–161.

106   Federal Reserve Bank of Cleveland, *Economic Trends,* June 1995, p. 15.

106   See David Folkerts-Landau and Takatoshi Ito, *et al.*, *International Capital Markets: Developments, Prospects, and Policy Issues* (Washington, DC: International Monetary Fund, August 1995), p. 18.

107   As Martin Mayer has suggested, the most important common law precedent goes against the banks. When interest-rate swaps between an English borough council and some London banks went the wrong direction, the borough refused to pay off, "arguing that playing in derivatives was something they had no legal authority to do, and the banks should have known it." See Martin Mayer, *The Bankers: The Next Generation* (New York: Truman Talley Books/Dutton, 1997), p. 330. The case won by the borough cost the British and American banks about $600 million.

Notes for pages 114–116

114   As reported by Gillian Tett, Capital Markets Editor, *Financial Times*, May 27, 2005.

116   Steel and Newman as quoted by Henny Sender, "Hedge Funds Nip at Wall Street, *Wall Street Journal*, May 26, 2005, p. C1.

Notes for pages 128–134

128   See James R. Hagerty, "Housing Prices Continue to Rise," *Wall Street Journal*, January 27, 2004, pp. D1, D2.

130   For more details on the report, see Hagerty, *Ibid.*

130   Quoted by Hagerty, *Ibid.*, p. D2.

130   As reported by James R. Hagerty and Ruth Simon, "As Prices Rise, Homeowners Go Deep in Debt to Buy Real Estate," *Wall Street Journal*, May 23, 2005, p. A1. See also David Wessel, "The Fed Starts to Show Concern at Signs of a Bubble in Housing, *Wall Street Journal*, May 19, 2005, pp. A1, A6.

134   The quotes are from Greenspan's testimony on "Government-Sponsored Enterprises" Before the Committee on Banking, Housing, and Urban Affairs, U.S. Senate, February 24, 2004.

Notes for pages 136–142

136   Deborah Rankin, "Personal Finance; Social Security Rises? Brace Yourself," *New York Times*, January 9, 1983, p. C19.

141   The complete story regarding Greenspan's marriage portfolio is told in the Washington AP Release by Dave Skidmore, "So, Where Does Greenspan Put His Money? Not in the Stock Market," August 19, 1998.

142   These data are reported in the Washington AP Release by Jeannine Aversa, "Greenspan Has Safe Investments," July 29, 2005.

Notes for pages 150–154

150   During this era, others have suggested that investment causes saving. See, as examples, Robert Eisner, *The Misunderstood Economy: What Counts and How to Count It* (Boston: Harvard Business School Press, 1995), pp. 33–41, Albert T. Sommers (with Lucie R. Blau), *The U.S. Economy Demystified*, Revised Edition (Lexington, Massachusetts: Lexington Books, 1988), pp. 55–59. Sommers, too, explains how net worth as savings can increase through the appreciation of financial assets, but

fails to find any cause in the wealth distribution or any adverse effects. Also, Nobelist William Vickery writes in a posthumous article: "Measures to promote individual saving produce exactly the opposite effect," in *Journal of Post Keynesian Economics*, Spring 1997, p. 499. For a textbook statement on the paradox of saving whereby attempts by people to save more lead both to a decline in output and to diminished saving, see Olivier Blanchard, *Macroeconomics* (Upper Saddle River, NJ: Prentice Hall, 1997), pp. 54–55.

150   These data and definitions of the terms, as well as similar data for other time periods appear in E. Ray Canterbery, "Reaganomics, Saving, and the Casino Effect," in James H. Gapinski (Editor), *The Economics of Saving* (Boston/Dordrecht/London: Kluwer Academic Publishers, 1993), p. 162.

150   See Canterbery, *Wall Street Capitalism* (New Jersey/London/Singapore: World Scientific, 2000).

152   Alternatively, the Fed's balance sheet measure of corporate savings (which include stock dividends and non-dividend cash payments) shows corporate savings actually turning negative during the late 1980s. See Canterbery, "Reaganomics, Saving, and the Casino Effect," *op. cit.*, pp. 165–166.

152   Total net amounts raised from corporate equities during 1995, 1996, and the first quarter of 1997 (annual rate) were −$17.7, −$18.5, and −$54.5 billion, respectively. That is, corporations bought back more stock than they issued. In contrast, net borrowing in corporate bonds was $197.0, $146.4, and $189.2, respectively, during the same periods. For the complete data, see *Federal Reserve Bulletin*, August 1997, Tables A37–A40.

154   These data are reported in Michael J. Fleming, "The Round-the-Clock Market for U.S. Treasury Securities," *Economic Policy Review, Federal Reserve Bank of New York*, July 1997, pp. 9–32. In addition to these transactions, the primary dealers on Wall Street also traded $18.3 billion *per day* in U.S. Treasury futures, $5.1 billion in forwards, and $7.8 billion in options.

Notes for pages 157–158

157 The Feldstein quotes are from Martin Feldstein, "Saving Social Security," *Wall Street Journal*, July 15, 2005, editorial page.

158 The Bernanke quotes are as reported by Greg Ip, "U.S. on Track for 3.4% Growth, White House Economist Says," *Wall Street Journal*, July 13, 2005, p. B2.

Notes for pages 160–167

160 The author has found great economic wisdom in Scott Fitzgerald. See E. Ray Canterbery and Thomas Birch, *F. Scott Fitzgerald: Under the Influence* (St. Paul, Minnesota: Paragon House, 2006).

162 The details appear in E. Ray Canterbery, *Wall Street Capitalism* (New Jersey/London/Singapore: World Scientific, 2000), chapter 14.

163 The details of my original proposal appear in Canterbery, *Wall Street Capitalism, op. cit.*, chapter 15.

164 Further details on the interest-free intra-government loan idea are found in Canterbery, *Wall Street Capitalism*, chapter 15. In the United States, S. Jay Levy and Walter M. Cadette of The Jerome Levy Economics Institute propose the establishment of a Federal Bank for Infrastructure Modernization (FBIM), which would buy and hold approximately $50 billion a year of zero-interest mortgage loans to state and local governments for capital investment in projects recommended by Congress and the president. The "deposits" created as liabilities of the FBIM would be held as assets by the Federal Reserve System. They suggest a maximum mortgage of 30 years, the period of repayment depending on the type of project, with the principal repaid in annual instalments.

166 Elsewhere, I, and others, have presented detailed plans for tax reform: A survey of the plans appear in E. Ray Canterbery, *The Making of Economics, Third Edition* (Belmont, CA: Wadsworth, 1987), chapter 17, and in the forthcoming *The Making of Economics, Fourth Edition: Vol. III, The Radical*

Assault (New Jersey/London/Singapore: World Scientific). An initial proposal appears in an article by the same author in "Tax Reform and Incomes Policy: A VATIP Proposal," *Journal of Post Keynesian Economics* 5 (Spring 1983), 430–439. A later, more detailed version of the plan appears in E. Ray Canterbery, Eric W. Cook, and Bernard A. Schmitt, "The Flat Tax, Negative Tax, and VAT: Gaining Progressivity and Revenue," *Cato Journal* (Fall 1985), 521–536 (based upon a paper given at the Conference on the Flat Tax Proposals, Florida State University, March 14, 1985). Embedded in these reforms is a new kind of incomes policy that would use tax incentives to limit wage and profits inflation, making it unnecessary to use monetary policy to cause recession and slow growth to limit inflation.

166   John Maynard Keynes, *The General Theory of Employment, Interest, and Money* (New York: Harcourt, Brace & World, 1965) [1936], p. 373.

167   *Ibid.*, p. 374.

INDEX